BOUNDLESS
2021

The anthology of the
Rio Grande Valley
International Poetry Festival

Edited by
Sarah Joy Thompson
Gabriel González Núñez
& Edward Vidaurre

FlowerSong Press

McAllen, Texas 78501

Copyright © 2021 FlowerSong Press

ISBN 978-1-953447-42-5:

Published by FlowerSong Press
in the United States of America.
www.flowersongpress.com

Set in Avenir

Typeset and design by Matthew Revert
www.matthewrevert.com

BOUNDLESS: 2020 the Anthology of the

RIO GRANDE VALLEY INTERNATIONAL POETRY FESTIVAL

FLOWERSONG
PRESS

Selected and Edited by
Edward Vidaurre
Sarah Joy Thompson
& Gabriel González Núñez

Rio Grande Valley
International Poetry Festival
www.valleypoetryfest.org

Boundless is the official anthology of the Rio Grande Valley
International Poetry Festival (VIPF), founded in 2008 by Daniel
García Ordaz and Brenda Nettles Riojas.

VIPF is held annually the last weekend in April in deep South Texas as
a celebration of National Poetry Month. Directed by Edward Vidaurre

Contents

INTRODUCTION

As the Rio Grande Valley International Poetry Festival kicks off its 14th annual celebration, we as coeditors look forward to showcasing the work of the authors who contributed to this year's anthology, *Boundless 2021*. The purpose of this anthology, like the Festival itself, has been to connect writers from around the globe, as many artists and poets are brought face to face through each page of poetry. When COVID-19 struck in early 2020, the Festival directors adapted, taking on the task of working around a virtual environment and adopting more of a virtual nature for the events and festivities. Now, in 2021, the Festival again will take place online. Perhaps because of the essential value of poetry, not even a global pandemic kept the Festival from missing a beat.

It was truly an honor to read the work that the contributing authors shared with the anthology, in terms of the diverse tones, registers, and themes. After careful reading and weighing, we selected the works that stood out, the pieces that sparked something within – that carried power and space to uplift those who endured through the hardships of a yearlong pandemic – and namely pieces with a coherent flow: beginning, middle, end. There were also works that ignited emotion, celebrated the many facets of human nature, and portrayed a clear voice and point of view. We wanted as many poems as possible that held water, so we gladly accepted work from new and emerging voices, along with work from seasoned writers.

For these reasons, it is fitting that the Festival's anthology be titled *Boundless*. Boundless. As in having no bounds. As in having no limits. Boundless. Limitless. Horizonless. The anthology is all of these things. The poems represent all of these things, and so do the poets who wrote them. Some of the poets hail from different parts of Mexico and the United States, as one would expect from an anthology born in the Borderlands between those two countries. In that spirit, we accepted poems in both English and Spanish. Even so, our poets come not just from these two countries but also from lands as different as Cyprus and El Salvador, India and Nigeria. They represent all of humanity in its boundless races, limitless worldviews, and horizonless experiences.

We trust you will enjoy reading these voices as much as we enjoyed receiving all of the poems and creating this selection for you. So grab a cup of hot chocolate or coffee or tea or what have you, get comfortable in your favorite place around the house, and dive into *Boundless 2021*.

Sarah Joy Thomson
Gabriel González Núñez

PRESENTACIÓN

Ahora que el Festival Internacional de Poesía del Río Grande da inicio a su decimocuarta edición anual, como coeditores nos entusiasma presentar la obra de los autores que han aportado sus composiciones a *Boundless 2021*, la antología de este año. La finalidad de esta edición antológica es la misma del festival, a saber, la de conectar a escritores de todo el mundo, lo cual hacemos página tras página de poesía. Cuando a principios de 2020 nos embistió la cóvid, los directores del festival se adaptaron, asumiendo el reto de efectuar todo en un entorno digital, y así le brindaron a los actos y festividades una naturaleza virtual, y ahora, en 2021, el festival nuevamente se realizará en línea. Tal vez por causa del valor esencial de la poesía, ni siquiera una pandemia mundial pudo conseguir que el festival perdiera el compás.

Para nosotros leer los trabajos de los autores que colaboraron con la antología fue un verdadero honor, un deleite de tonos, registros y temas. Tras leer y sopesar detenidamente, seleccionamos las obras que más nos llamaron la atención, las composiciones que movieron algo en nuestro interior —las que tenían el poder y creaban el espacio para elevar a quienes han sufrido las dificultades de una pandemia que va para un año largo—, y en concreto, poemas que fluían de forma coherente, desde el principio pasando por el medio para llegar al fin. También seleccionamos obras que despiertan emociones, que celebran las distintas facetas de la naturaleza humana y que exhiben una voz marcada y un punto de vista inequívoco. Buscamos incluir la mayor cantidad de poemas que se tienen en pie, así que aceptamos tanto obras de voces emergentes como trabajos de autores establecidos.

Por estos motivos tiene sentido que la antología del festival se llame *Boundless*. Esta palabra se puede traducir como «sin límites». Ilimitado. Infinito. Inagotable. La antología es todo esto. Los poemas representan todo esto, así como lo hacen sus poetas. Algunos de los autores provienen de distintas partes de Estados Unidos y México, como es de esperarse tratándose de una antología nacida en la Zona Fronteriza entre estos dos países. Con ese espíritu, hemos incluido obras tanto en castellano como en inglés. Mirando más allá, nuestros poetas provienen no solo de esos dos países sino también de tierras tan dispares como Chipre y El Salvador o como la India y Nigeria. Representan a toda la humanidad con sus ilimitadas razas, infinitas formas de ver el mundo e inagotables vivencias.

Tenemos la expectativa de que usted, estimado lector, disfrute de la lectura de estas voces tanto como nosotros disfrutamos de recibir los poemas y armar para usted esta selección. Así que sírvase una taza de chocolate caliente o de café o té o lo que sea, póngase cómodo en su rincón preferido de la casa y sumérjase en *Boundless 2021*.

Gabriel González Núñez
Sarah Joy Thomson

Dedication

In honor of:
Jan Seale. 2012 Texas State Poet Laureate, McAllen, Texas
Emmy Pérez, 2020 Texas Poet Laureate, McAllen, Texas
Rodney Gomez, 2020-2021 City of McAllen Poet Laureate
In memoriam:
Dr. Gloria E. Anzaldúa
Jovita González
Dr. Américo Paredes
Rául R. Salinas
Trinidad Sánchez, Jr.
Roque Dalton
Amiri Baraka
Roberto De La Torre
Jesús Pérez
Lawrence Ferlinghetti

you
couldn't
handle me,
darling

Unwritten

1

2

3

4

5

-Sandra Dolores Gómez-Amador

---

1 I am not writing about your blue fingertips, cold froth against my skin that night of january.
2 Nor am I writing of the small horizontal scar on your nose tip, a memory of your first childhood home.
3 I do not write about your deep voice late at night, a warm bolt of tenderness that pierces through my shattered body
4 Nor do I write of your ghost, a burst of amber light that silently haunts my empty bed.
5 I am writing of this thing I feel inside— this thing that fills my chest with fires that I do not know if I will ever be capable of extinguishing.

Welcome

Dappled
Shadows shifting
close, ebb-flow power grows.
Shadow spell, magic, brilliant edge —
of things
Power
Of a deep kiss
Conjures balance, pregnant
with purple blues. She feels at sea —
unmoored
Stories
in torn fire
on the great river road.
This is where the rescue folks come —
shining
Wild rose
Watch out for snakes
They'll steal your heart away.
Without caring about pieces —
they've torn
He kissed
the deer antler
Whistle, then blew for luck.
His present calling for his past —
With her

-Odilia Galván Rodríguez

Gloria Mundi

Mountains unseam,
split, spit red thunder, all life
in excess: the drop
of milk rises pearly
to nipple's peak
and trembles for
a mouth: live rain.

What need does
beauty have of us:
this kernel of corn
holds within itself
every milpa through time, cracked in mouse's teeth
flea upon its back
wanders aspen glade of fur: obsidian ceremonial dagger
driven in, sips
crimson platelets
from the same heart as mine.

Virgen de Guadalupe pray for us,
Tonantzin, pray for us,
Malinche, pray for us,
Tlazolteotl, pray for us.
Santa Sabina, pray for us.
Soldadera, pray for us,
Hechizera, pray for us.
Profesora, pray for us.
Despeinada, pray for us.
Chola, pray for us.

Sor Juana, pray for us.
Bruja, pray for us.

Poets pray for us.
Abuela, pray for us.
Now and in the hour of our death
In the glory of what
You have given us,
Amen.

-Luis Alberto Urrea

heavy handed

Ms. Green insists I will never learn cursive,
that my hand will not conform, the fat cushion
of my palm dragging across the newsprint.

My HB pencils the secret of small drawings.
It's how I learned shading. All the pads of my fingertips
clothed in iridescent coal.

But handwritten words, with their rounded joints, should be clear.
Erasing makes it all worse.

Ms. Green threatens me. She says I'll never
be allowed to write with the ballpoint pens if
I can't lose the sluggishness and lift my hand.

And so I become this crooked thing,
my arm in an awkward arch, my head at an angle,
my fingers tight around the pencil, writing over and over again

> *The quick brown fox jumps over the lazy dog.*

Until I am all hand and all hurt. Until my hand begs that I stop.

I take pages and pencils home with me,
trying again and again, each time praying
the words – overwritten mush –
are transformed into one elegant spiral of graphite,
dark as night, encircling the brilliant stars.

-jo reyes boitel

0

"Gira el carrusel del cero y sigue sonando el mar,
estar arriba o abajo es lo que menos importa,
nunca me siento solo en el oleaje intenso de la escritura,
nadar quiere mi llama hacia la otra orilla."
-Samuel Noyola

I

Entregado al arte de mancillar la carne me vuelvo parte de un paisaje urbano.
Decidido, únicamente, a conversar con la maleza que ha roto el pavimento,
olvido la lengua materna,

aprendiendo la universalidad del silencio.

II

No me pregunten por los nombres propios. Aquí todos nos llamamos de la misma forma.
Bautizados por el desprecio de quien nos pronuncia,
aprendimos a reconocernos por toda la ternura
que no supimos entregar.

III

El invierno es la época
donde las charcas

conocen nuestra sed

y espero dejar de amanecer
eternamente anochecido
para poder recorrer el pavimento

sin miedo de convertirme en parte de él.

-Javier Fuentes Vargas

No country for old men

"De madrugada, cuando los hombres sueñan, salgo a buscar la plaza."
-Samuel Noyola.

I

Busco la plaza,
la fuente,
el árbol.

Eso es lo aparente.

En realidad
busco los ojos de cualquiera,
el deseo que hay detrás de la moneda
en el fondo del agua,
el pájaro que baja al suelo, no en busca de semillas, sino de mis manos.

II

Dañé mis manos vueltas barro
antes que los pájaros bajasen
 a buscar entre ellas
una piadosa muerte.

No soportaría ahogar el canto
ni la danza conmovida.

III

Estas estaciones no están hechas para mis años.

Ya no puedo soñar
con la plenitud del vuelo de las palomas,
sólo con mis manos alrededor de sus cuellos,
como buscando arrebatar la vacuidad de sus ojos
que me recuerdan tanto a la inocencia perdida.

IV

La inocencia
es lo único que verdaderamente se extraña.

Si la vejez no es como una nueva infancia,
es entonces una larga avenida
que se transita sin querer la vida
ni esperar la muerte.

-Javier Fuentes Vargas

Desierto

I

El desierto no entiende de lenguas, no está hecho para la sed y la agonía.

II

Los pasos:
el efímero legado de nuestra estancia. Los nombres son otra especie de pasos,
una repetición que condiciona nuestra identidad.

III

El desierto es una diminuta mentira
en la boca de mi madre.
No tiene idea de toda la arena que acusa
al nombrar mi rostro
como un sol despiadado.

IV

Un cactus erguido
como un obelisco a la esperanza arrulla mi necio sentido orientación.

V

Si alguna vez hubo esperanza
de reencontrar el camino,
abandonada quedó a la sombra de las dunas.
Nada es peor en un largo viaje
que cargar con un peso muerto

-Javier Fuentes Vargas

Whirling Log

Elias was grading the washed-out dirt road for the Bureau. An unexpected summer storm passed through yesterday and access to the reservation was limited. Just after sunrise, a distraught Navajo man approached the chapter house. His crops had been destroyed and he wanted to ask about his dreams. *Where do they go to die?* A place where gods commune was already being prepared with sands and powders colored with cornmeal, charcoal, and sandstone. The design elements of the sacred mandala were laid out, guided by spirits of the Four Sacred Mountains. The healing would soon begin. Mother was splitting kindling, preparing the last of kneeldown bread and squash blossoms to place in the *horno*. The dreamer was hollowing out a log under the watchful gaze of the gods. He prayed carry me down river, watch over me as I seek to find sustenance, to restore life in beauty. The river's current was swift and treacherous, full of obstacles, detours, and demons. He knew time had lost all meaning as he was pulled underneath the relentless, rushing water. By the grace of the benevolent gods, he was suddenly thrown out of the log and landed on the shore of a calm lake. He wandered until finding a whirling cross with two *yeis* standing on each arm. He gave thanks and they handed him a gift of seeds containing the promise of a new harvest. He was now free to return home. The chapter house floor was carefully swept, restored to its natural state. The sands, powders, and minerals were carried out and returned to the earth at the base of a blackened tree that had been struck by lightning. Elias angled the shiny blade of his grader to begin his final pass. As he looked back and admired his work, he saw a man nearby planting seeds and he smiled, *life is restored in beauty*.

-Kenneth Johnson

One Nation Under God

They came on horseback
over the Appalachian Highlands,
building lean-tos and log cabins,
hunting deer and wild turkeys with
smooth bore muskets and long rifles,
growing sweet corn, wheat, and flax,
stitching homespun clothing while
farmers homesteaded Free Soil
and armed militias watched over
the birth of one nation under God.

Cherokee and Seminole nations
subjugated to a Trail of Tears,
guided by Colts and Remingtons,
their destiny was made manifest.
Winchesters and Springfields won
corrals and streets of the frontier,
the heart and soul of America,
as it awakened to a new morning,
the fire and deafening thunder in
the name of one nation under God

I have a dream the dreamer said,
Let freedom ring from every hill,
every street, every state, every city
while they ask when will you be
satisfied in the blood stained streets
of El Paso, Detroit, Atlanta, Chicago,
New Orleans, Orlando, Las Vegas?

When will justice roll down like waters,
when will these truths be self-evident
in one nation under God?

-Kenneth Johnson

Journey to Mictlan

I enter here naked and blind,
worn and ragged I will traverse
flailing mountains, lakes of fire,
bitter winds and arrows of glass

I will fend off your screaming dogs,
trudge through snow that never ends
I will navigate rivers of blood in a
relentless rain of invisible sorrows

I will offer my skin to be flayed
on an altar of obsidian knives
I will split open my chest to be
ravaged by rabid, raging beasts

I will stare into the jaguar's soul
deep inside black endless canyons
I will mix bones, blood, and maize,
melding morning and midnight stars

I will dine on bread, honey, and nopal,
cacao sweetened with dream flowers
I will sing and fly as a hummingbird
in a wondrous land of eternal spring

-Kenneth Johnson

La Frontera

Take the butterfly farm: take the trees
and paths and every animal's habitat,
take too the historic La Lomita Chapel,
take its wrought-iron cross and plaster.

Hoard the asphalt used for paved roads.
Keep it from colonias built fast,
take mothers' chances for light and water,
take their mothers' chance to see them.

Make it so their sons and daughters
never get to college, how dare they cross
as children—take their ambition, grind it
with the valley lemons they pick.

The Spanish led the conquering pack,
meaning eagle stomps snake and laughs,
meaning America comes to steal
that San Antonio mission, their turn

to laugh, to confiscate deeds in El Valle—
now even the Spanish feel the palms' heat.
Today the brown fence blocks brown faces,
obscuring the lives of grandmothers waiting.

-Robert J. Cavazos

Una piedra,

el lecho marino
alzado en hombros
por el fuego.
La lluvia,
la lluvia del martes,
la lluvia del domingo,
el diluvio universal de todos los días,
la tormenta de los siglos
de los siglos de los siglos,
la lluvia, el tiempo,
que cae sobre la piedra
y se acumula
y la socava
y la erosiona
y la carcome
y la lame
y la enmudece
y la acaricia
y la recorre
y la derrite
y no la agrieta
la perfora
la dibuja
la recita
le traza en las manos
las líneas
el canto
la memoria.
La gravedad,

la sutil fuerza del silencio,
hacia abajo,
por entre la piedra,
gota a gota
el silencio,
la piedra,
un río.

Un cuerpo,
dos cuerpos,
tres mil
y ciento cincuenta mil cuerpos
y el río
y los cuerpos
y los ciento cincuenta mil ríos
la piedra
la suma del tiempo
sobre todos los cuerpos,
el mar.

-Julio Serrano Echeverría

(Translated by Laura August)

One stone,

the sea bed
raised on shoulders
by the fire.
The rain
the rain of Tuesday
the rain of Sunday
the great Flood at the end of days
the storm of the centuries
of the centuries of the centuries
the rain, the time
that falls about the stone
and that gathers
and ruins it
and erodes it
and consumes it
and licks it
and makes it mute
and caresses it
and returns to it
and melts it
and does not split it
punctures it
draws it
recites it
and traces in the hands
the lines
the song

the memory.
The gravity
the subtle force of the silence,
from below,
which enters the stone,
drop by drop
the silence,
the stone,
a river.

One body,
two bodies,
three thousand
and one hundred fifty thousand bodies
and the river
and the bodies
and the hundred fifty thousand rivers
the stone
the sum of time
above all the bodies,
the sea

-Julio Serrano Echeverría

Tabula rasa

Conozco este espacio.
Acá era la infancia
y algunos de los jardines de los amigos.
Lo conozco de una bicicleta pequeña,
lo conozco de algún balcón,
de una caminata un día cualquiera,
de cualquier tiempo,
digo de un tiempo: el nuestro.
Conozco este lugar
y es posible pensarlo como un cuarto vacío,
vaciado,
el cuarto de los desfiles,
el cuarto de los solados.
Conozco este lugar, me reconozco.
Aquí fui soldado raso
cargando sacos de arena,
cargando sacos de harina,
cargando cuerpos como quintales.
Me reconozco acá soldado
y acá cuerpo,
el cuerpo muerto
enterrado quizá bajo las planchas de cemento
donde cae la lluvia.
Conozco este espacio
y brotan raíces a mis piernas,
ellas conocen la voz bajo la tierra,
saben el grito,
saben el gemido brutal,
la oscuridad subterránea;

lo saben las raíces,
lo saben mis piernas
y llueve sobre las planchas de cemento
donde estarán enterradas las flores del enamorado.
Me reconozco abrazando a esos cuerpos,
corriendo por las paredes,
escalando por los troncos viejos
de los árboles que arrancamos
y no me basta el lugar,
me basta la memoria
y el puño que aprieta el cielo
como la lluvia que insiste,
la lluvia.
No sé qué decir de los agujeros en las ventanas,
no sé que contarles de la manera en que el agua
agrieta los metales en el techo.
No sé bien qué decir de los pequeños charcos
que reflejan el cielo gris,
el cielo más gris que desde este lugar reconocemos.
No sé muy bien qué contarles de las paredes,
de los animales que salen de los pequeños agujeros,
no sé muy bien qué, pero lo reconozco,
pero nos reconozco acá corriendo,
pero nos reconozco acá gritando,
susurrando palabras de amor,
como las flores que enterramos,
reconozco este lugar.
y reconozco su olvido.
Reconozco tu voz cuando me llama
y despiertan de nuevo los cuerpos que corrían apresurados
a tomar el tren.

Dicen, y no me consta,

dicen que acá sonaban las campanillas de los relojes.

Reconozco en realidad algunos cuadros en el suelo,

tumbas quizás,

huertos quizás,

reconozco mis manos sepultadas,

reconozco los pasos firmes que pasan sobre nuestras cabezas,

reconozco una voz,

una que canta suavecito antes de que se apague el fuego.

Podría reconocer el olor de nuestros cuerpos,

podría reconocer el olor de aquellos cuerpos,

los que cargamos como sacos de arena,

como sacos de tiempo que se vacían.

Podría reconocer los cuerpos,

casi podría nombrarlos,

aunque no pueda decirte en realidad como me llamo,

ni sepa decirte el color que me recuerdan estas paredes,

este tiempo,

las palabras con las que me gustaría explicarte

en qué nos hemos convertido,

y qué nos hizo este lugar.

El poema fue escrito en la antigua estación del ferrocarril de Xelajú, Guatemala. La estación fue convertida en una base militar que durante la guerra civil en Guatemala fue utilizada para secuestrar, torturar y muy probablemente ejecutar presos políticos.

La acción consistió en llegar al hangar principal sin una idea previa, sentarse, escribir desde cero este poema a partir de la experiencia en el lugar y finalmente leerlo ahí. Justo en medio de la lectura del poema una lluvia torrencial cayó sobre el techo de esta antigua zona militar.

-Julio Serrano Echeverría

Tabula rasa

(translated by Fernando Feliu Moggi)

I know this space.
This is where childhood was
and some of my friends' yards.
I know it from riding a small bike,
I know it from looking out of some balcony,
from walking by it on any given day.
from anytime,
I mean from one time: ours.
I know this place
which can be thought of as an empty room,
drained,
the parade hall,
the soldiers' quarters.
I know this place, I know myself.
I was a corporal here
hauling sandbags,
hauling bags of flour,
hauling bodies that weighed a ton.
I know myself a soldier here
and here a corpse,
the dead body
perhaps buried under the cement slabs
where the rain falls.
I know this space
And roots grow out of my legs,
they know the voices underground,
they know the scream,

they know the brutal moan,
the subterranean darkness;
the roots know it,
my legs know it
and it rains on the cement slabs
where the lover's flowers must be buried.
I know myself embracing those bodies,
running through the walls,
climbing the old trunks
of the trees we pulled
and the place is not enough,
my memory is enough
and the fist gripping the sky
like the insisting rain,
the rain.
I don't know what to say about the holes in the windows,
I don't know what to tell you about the way water
cracks the metal on the roof.
I'm not sure what to say about the tiny puddles
reflecting the gray sky,
the grayest sky we can know over here.
I am not too sure of what to tell you about the walls,
of the animals poking out of the small holes,
I am not too sure about what, but I know it,
I know us here, running
I know us here, screaming,
whispering sweet nothings,
like the flowers we buried,
I know this place,
I know its forgetting.
I know its voice when it calls me

and the bodies that rushed about
to take the train awake.
They say, though I have not seen it,
they say here the tiny bells of clocks would chime.

Actually, I know some squares on the ground,
perhaps graves,
perhaps gardens,
I know my buried hands,
I know the stern steps marching over our heads,
I know a voice,
one singing gently before the fire goes out.
I knew the smell of our bodies,
I knew the smell of those bodies,
those we hauled like sandbags

like bags of time emptying out.
I knew the bodies,
I could almost name them,
although I can really, barely tell you what my name is,
and I could not tell you what color these walls remind me of,
this time,
the words with which I'd like to explain to you
what we've become,
and what made us this place.

The poem was written at the old railroad station in Xelajú, Guatemala, which was turned into a military barracks during the Guatemalan civil war and used in the kidnapping, torture, and probably execution of political prisoners. The action consisted of arriving at the main hangar without any preconceived ideas, sitting down, writing this poem from scratch based on the experience of the place, and, finally, reading it there. Right in the middle of the reading, a torrential rain fell on the roof of this former military quarters.

-Julio Serrano Echeverría

Central América

III

La memoria es una travesía,
caminaremos el mar,
caminaremos la selva,
caminaremos el desierto;
piedra sobre piedra
para recordarnos,
correremos en dirección opuesta
para tensar el corazón,
para sacarle las palabras al pecho.
Desde estas ventanas de autobús
nos irás recordando poco a poco,
poco a poco te iremos recordando.

Es de noche
como las noches infranqueables donde solo había fuego,
aparece en el asfalto iluminado por las luces del pullman
una familia sentada alrededor de la hoguera.

Las ventanas atestiguan dentro del bus,
una danza de ojos vidriosos que sueñan,
recuerdan el desierto sin saberlo,
siguiendo las estaciones,
recolectando alimentos.
Recuerdan el fuego
y la innombrable llama que les ardía por dentro.

Alguien despierta en medio de la noche,

hay luna y la arena es azul,
polvo de estrella,
alguien despierta, recio, pronuncia para sí
¡Siempre hemos perseguido a la comida
porque siempre hemos tenido hambre!,
y las ventanas atestiguan
hacia dentro,
hacia afuera,
esta insaciable búsqueda de abrigo
para no llegar con manos vacías
al lecho de la muerte.

Alguien despierta en medio del amanecer,
soñaba que hacía burbujas de jabón en un parque
pero ya no lo sueña más.
Es el día
y el desierto se descascara como una serpiente seca,
cada piedra, un árbol
cada escama, una pluma.
Las ventanas atestiguan ahora
a una niña y su memoria,
magma adormecido de la tierra
atravesando el tiempo en erupción.

Militares. Policías. Gente apresurada, triste y con miedo. Trajes de muchos colores. Tejidos y textiles en todos lados. Mujeres, hombres y niños vendiendo comida y refrescos a través de las ventanas en las paradas de bus. Gente y casas pobres. El color de los cultivos. Campesinos a lo lejos arando trabajando la tierra. Montañas. Grandes extensiones de tierra, tierra ociosa. Más campesinos. Canastos. Animales dentro de canastos. Perros callejeros. Niñas y niños pequeñitos con mecapal a la frente cargando enormes atados de leña, sacos con verduras. Tristeza. Gente enojada. Mujeres embarazadas cargando bebés a la espalda o caminando junto a ellos. Mujeres adolescentes aseñoradas, envejecidas. Mujeres con delantales. Muchos cables eléctricos, muchos nidos sobre cables eléctricos. Más gente apresurada corriendo. Ayudantes de bus gritando. Basura. Niños llenos de mocos. Niños llorando enojados y hermosos. Muchachos jugando a las patadas en las calles. Borrachos. La ciudad, cantinas, changarros. Anuncios de Coca Cola, anuncios de cerveza, anuncios de lugares turísticos, anuncios gigantes con mujeres semidesnudas que no son como nosotras. Pacas. Buses a gran velocidad, todo en estrépito. Caos, dolor.

La niña abre todas las ventanas del bus,
y no grita,
respira.

-Julio Serrano Echeverría

Central América

(Translated by Fernando Feliu-Moggi)

III

Memory is a journey
we will walk the sea
we will walk the jungle
we will walk the desert
stone on stone
to remember ourselves
we will run in the opposite direction
to strain our heart
to get words out of our chest.
From these bus windows
you will remember us little by little
little by little we will remember you.

It is night
like the impassable nights where there was only fire
on the asphalt lit up by the lights of the Pullman
emerges a family sitting around the bonfire.

The windows bear witness inside the bus
to a dance of dreaming glassy eyes
that remember the desert without knowing

following the seasons
collecting foodstuffs.
They remember the fire
and the unspeakable flame that burned inside them.

Someone awakens in the middle of the night
the moon is out the sand is blue
stardust
someone awakens and states harshly inward
We've always chased food
because we've always been hungry!
and the windows bear witness
inwards
outward
to this insatiable pursuit of shelter
in order not to arrive empty-handed
to our deathbed.

Someone awakens mid-dawn
They dreamed they blew soap bubbles in a park
but they are no longer dreaming.
It is day
and the desert peels like a dry snake
every stone a tree
every scale a feather.
The windows bear witness now
to a girl and her memory
sleepy magma of the earth
crossing the erupting time

Military. Cops. Hurried people sad and scared. Suits of many colors. Fabrics and textiles everywhere. Women men and children selling food and sodas through the windows at bus stops. Poor people and houses. The color of the crops. Peasants in the distance plowing working the land. Mountains. Large tracts of land idle land. More peasants. Baskets. Animals inside baskets. Stray dogs. Little boys and girls with mecapales on their forehead carrying large bundles of wood bags with vegetables. Sadness. Angry people. Pregnant women carrying babies on their backs or walking alongside them. Teenage women aged woman-like. Women with aprons. Many electrical wires, many nests on electrical wires. More hurried people running. Bus assistants yelling. Garbage. Snotty children. Angry and beautiful children crying. Teens playing kick in the street. Drunkards. The city saloons shops. Coca Cola ads beer ads tourist spot ads giant ads with semi-naked women who are not like us. Bales. Buses at high speeds, everything's a racket. Chaos pain.

The girl opens all the window in the bus
and doesn't scream
she breathes.

-Julio Serrano Echeverría

you are
my
mind

DNA

I follow the transience of multiple races,
itch to move every muffled,
rain-soaked Saturday.

Out the window, I dream of relocating
back to San Antonio,
buying a cottage,

then traveling further, to southern Italy,
Northern Mexico, and then Spain,
the diaspora of Jewish Europe.

I seek word of Hispanic educational gains,
indigenous arts culinary and visual,
Italian Americans in politics,

I fade in and out of each culture—
rain reaching different surfaces,
just as soon moved.

-Robert J. Cavazos

Recipe

I.   Avoid cheap nonstick pans:
Pour oil
      smoke each first and last memory

Set down meat
      don't forget to flinch when flipped

II.   Pronounce like a hangover prayer:
huevos con chorizo
      let yourself crack and scramble

salsa y queso fresco
      equal parts red, white, and brown

III.   Fully-cooked words:
Ground beef in the pot
      holiday mornings watching TV parades

Italian herbs and spices
      your Mom-Mom tells you a family secret

IV.   When away from home:
Make mistakes at grocery stores
      get the wrong white Mexican cheese

Decide between foreign songs
      forget to fill tomato cans with water

V.   Remember this feeling:

Paesanos on the Riverwalk
> linen tablecloths and ducks floating by

El Rafa's Cafe on the Westside
> bright colored walls, thick carne guisada.

-Robert J. Cavazos

PRECIPICE

Gladly say goodbye
To the proven nightmare,
These past
Four years—

The precipice
On which I stand
Is crowded with eagerness
Waiting on cures
For both viruses.

The one
Ailing bodies,
The one
Extinguishing love.

Smooth transition
Into another era,
Focus of everybody's
Endogenic wishes, appealing even to my jaded self.
When I close my eyes,
I hear the popular song of

"What Now?"

-Dee Allen

Breaking the Taco Shell

Breaking a thought like breaking wind
Noisily bound by mental-phorical chains
Super invisible to my dark, brown eyes
Appearing only to my ever-busy mind
Playing *tonto* tricks on unassuming me
Making me roll my Mexican "r"s
Or forcing others to make fun of me
When I say *Chi*cago or *ch*air
Making me think that
The Progressive Girl Flo
Needs a good, bare-butt spanking
For selling car insurance
To would-be stupid, drunk drivers
Making me think that
The whole wide, wicked world is burning up
Melting my mestizo, stone-cold heart
Then serving it up well done
On a porcelain, white plate
Disguised as a flat, fat ovary
With the ghostly figure of La Virgin De Guadalupe
Stamped to the bottom of the delicate platter
Locked into infinity as a holy-relic, EBay item
Locked by those chains of my clumsy brain
Wrapped around a taco shell of a skull
Encasing rancid beans burning my mind

-Juan Manuel Pérez

Chupa-Ku, Volume XIII: No. 61-65

imagination
the only proof between us
fear, or not to fear

you believe in ghosts
I, in *el chupacabra*
which makes us less scared

no matter what size
monster will be monster
chupacabra lives

the dead grass crumbles
as the grey beast stalks its prey
under cool moon light

ever stop to think
if *el chupacabra* cares
whether it is real

-Juan Manuel Pérez

PORTAL

He held onto the little scull he'd brought from Austin
The new neighbor boy with few friends stood next to me on The silt of
Galveston shores

In the fading twilight
I could only make out the glowing ferris wheel
Pleasure Pier standing off in the distance

His eyes were glazed from the alcohol and I remember
Not wanting to leave him on the edge like the others

When he got the rowboat steady in the turning basin
He gestured for me to get on

In some ways I felt like *Sheila Mant*
As I settled into the cushions near the bow

Soon we floated around the curve of this pseudo-canal
And onto the shores of Bolivar

He asked me if I knew the legend--
Of the General's house that stood somewhere in this peninsula

I imagined a man and his diary as he lay dying in exile
The water is clearer this side of the gulf
And his eyes are gleaming midnight blue
I'd never seen pupils so wide

He talked of mythic treasure as if I were the pirate queen of Illyria I knew he was trying to forget his parents' divorce

We sat on the rocks and watched the sunset
I pressed my eyes into the horizon searching

        For a way to ask if he was alright

I watched the current shift as the moon rose
Pulling tides as she flew into her bed of stars

     He seemed more relaxed under blue moonlight

I kissed his salty lips as the dinghy floated
Shifting in Poseidon's open mouth

Until we drifted back to that familiar pier and
The sound of girlish shrieks and carnival rides broke our daze

 I think of how my Khalu describes the moment between waves when
Time is suspended

  in the disturbance of moving from equilibrium to peak and
back again

Until we are pulling his boat onto land
My Wetherell fantasy has popped like kernels in the pier's concession
stand And we

       remember this day as a dream

-Tamara Al-Qaisi-Coleman

VELASCO

The Lute's plucked songs carry across the Schooner/ Drifting away from the Crescent City/ The singer is a man of many gifts/ Watching the pirates clutch to worn photos of fallen women/ Cholera bouncing between sniffle and cough/ The troubadour can see the ghouls of dead generals come aboard/ Signaling their arrival in Velasco/ This is his curse/ To write songs from the stories of dead men/ Their last breaths become meter/ His voice is an echo across/ This land that once belonged to giants/ Who roamed free among the islands/ Until they became fish/ The ghosts whisper secrets of the 112/ The ancient Gods disguised among them/ The tale of the rabbit who gave his body to feed the feathered serpent/ Now remembered/ Silhouette pressed against the moon's light/ "For all people and all times"/ The poet strums his steps through the old fort/ Telling tales of soldiers who haunt this island/ It is here he hears the voices of the massacred/ Souls floating across the breeze from Goliad/ Brother killing brother for power of Presidio la Baha/ Their moans speak of their curse/ By Tecciztecatl's cowardice/ Moonlight dimmed by a hare/ Until he reaches the grand hotel that sits against this Gulf/ His melody becomes/ Of the dove who brought the Chief a grain of dry sand/ The Great Flood receded/ His song brings sunlight to this bay/ Here he can listen for the stories of his children/ Their bodies lost in the depths/

-Tamara Al-Qaisi-Coleman

THE RAVEN, THE BAYOU, AND THE WILLOW

When Momma came home from the hospital her sisters whispered in the corner

The second *bint zina*
          she brought into this house of sin.

Your hands were so small they barely wrapped around my 8-year-old finger.
          The ravens flock to the old willow who breathes a sigh of
          relief
when her favorite one is settled into her lance-shaped leaves.
          You used to watch the flood-rain pour as the willow wept, your name was
     Annabelle and we lived in this house on the Brazos.

Birds flying always reminds me of Poe how I miss the
                         little bird that perched on our willow.
          The river, the bayou, and the neighbor's boat before the flood came and washed it
away. They said a swarm of birds flew into our house years after I left
          and you found your soulmate drunk at the neighborhood bar at 19.

Their feathers bloodied by glass-- cracking beaks as they warned
                         You never could sit still

The day you died I was walking the dog
                    Weary of golf course bridges

They stand uneven on stone sustained by old rotten planks
                              Your face floated like the souls in Acheron's waters
I imagined Atropos cutting your thread as
                    your body sunk to the bottom of the river

-Tamara Al-Qaisi-Coleman

Infancias perdidas

A todos los niños explotados, sin infancia.

En la edad de las risas y los juegos
 aprendieron a ser peones de barro
sobre el tablero de la muerte. Allí, lejos,
golpeaban con barras de hierro
sobre las leyes del tiempo, entre las rocas.
Lentamente, con gran esfuerzo, fueron llenando
 con pedazos de vida las calderas del infierno.
De sol a sol. Allí, a lo lejos y fuera del tiempo,
transportando las piedras y los días.
En sus manos estaban impresas, a fuego,

las marcas del esclavo, la existencia anónima,
la penuria de un tiempo sin infancia
atrapado en el barro del invierno.

En sus rostros renegridos brillaba una sonrisa
que no mitigaba el dolor de la inocencia perdida.
La cantera fue su escuela y hoy es su casa.
Su único juego fue escapar del hambre.
Aún siguen llorando al niño que no fueron.

-José Luis García Herrera

One world not three

"One world is enough for all of us."
-Sting

Amanece cada día en nuestro mundo,
sólo en un mundo, no en tres. Cada día,
 tras leer el periódico,
me pregunto qué razones justifican

que unas vidas valgan más y otras valgan menos.
No entiendo que hagamos de la muerte violenta
un acto cotidiano, que una mano ensangrentada
—flor de vida contra el viento del odio—
merezca sólo la mención de un frío comentario.
Y en las carreteras del mar mil sueños
cruzan a diario el filo salvaje del agua,
dejando atrás las jornadas sedientas del desierto,
el desgarro del hambre, el oscuro silencio
de una muerte callada.

Sólo conozco un mundo, injusto sí, pero nuestro.

Un mundo, una tierra, bajo el mismo sol y las estrellas.
Y deseo que en él haya espacio para todos,
en una torre de Babel con las puertas abiertas,
con manos abiertas a la esperanza,
con manos que sellan solidaridad en el esfuerzo,
que comparten la manta de los sueños.

-José Luis García Herrera

Passion

Everybody hides a secret passion.
Questioned by a psychologist,
I would have to confess:
"It is books that caused this fervour.
Books generate
an almost erotic passion in me,
awake a wild craving.
The silky, soft feeling of paper,
the rustling of the sides,
captivate me,
I get hooked on the text,
the warming book in my hands,
carry it with me wherever I go,
a community of fate,
longing for more,
pledge eternal fidelity,
a treasure that has so much to say,
and I have so many questions.
He who reads lives,
he who lives loves.

'4 am' is poet's time
I hear no bells chime
only the gentle move of leaves
and the flap of moth's wings.

-Eduard Schmidt-Zorner

On a new page.

Before my mind's eye
an idea, maybe a crazy one,
born from a dream on a restless night.

I woke up and put it on paper.
Words were whispered,
light as a feather, free as a bird,
words which go astray or into oblivion
if not written down instantly.

Some of them ruffle their feathers
and are soon forgotten
others lead to serious type cases,
letter after letter, typesetting.

Word-infatuated as I am,
meandering between lines,
densely written rows of notes,
illegible in the morning then.

What began remains unfinished.
Worn words, worn down, worn out,
or remain silent, leave no trace.
Evergreen word-tirades pass quickly,
they wither or manifest themselves,
become a cuckoo's egg in the composition,
unfit for epic proliferation.

'Age-shrewd' I turn the hourglass.

As wordsmith too loud the forging,
I weave with a light hand as
weaver of words,
to lie to the time, to interlace the minutes,
to form poems that cast no shadows.

-Eduard Schmidt-Zorner

Verses in greenhouses

Lyrical seedlings have many gardeners,
those who sow finely and in equal distance
others dig straight furrows,
those who, with a swift sweeping motion
scatter the seeds against the wind,
others are breeders who plan carefully
make the seeds sprout with patience,
some prepare the earth meticulously,
compress, level, scarify,
lay out flower beds, draw lines.

This all asks for rules,
which soon will be neglected and broken.
Syllable counters love the gardener's trade,
multicoloured fruits, as alliterations,
cross-, and end rhymes are created,
laboriously matching flower with bower
or roses with meadows
to put us in a lyrical mood.

I lean the rake against the fence
and take a rest.
Some things are rooted in flowerpots
or are disposed of in anthologies
until mildew settles
on the evergreen question.

-Eduard Schmidt-Zorner

Pelican in the Pandemic

This morning I wondered if you would fly into the window
confused, seeking safe shelter.

The wind was so close,
the water moving thunderstruck under your wings.

I wondered what sea fowl
you held in your bellows of a beak.

Heaviest of flying birds, air sacs breathing in your bones,
lightening your heft, your load.

You take refuge on the marble sill,
webs dangling over the edge.

Your breast is wounded
Opened to the salt breezes

You have been feeding your young
on your own blood offering during this scarcity of food.

Beak piercing your chest, again and again,
a self-inflicted opening of feather and flesh.

You are a banquet of ceremonial wine,
a feast of red river freshwater droplets

You gather them up,
urge them to suckle long and deep.

The lightning startles you,
shakes you from your landlocked perch.

I watch you take flight, magical
and exhausted in your buoyancy.

-Marianne Peel

maria, maria

we whisper secrets in the night, caressing shadows
holding onto our dreams
looking up at them -
an array displayed.
we cling on to each other on the bed.

smiling, waiting for that coffee in the morning.
you point out your shoes in this one and i smile.
my grip tightens.

this is the world, baby.
one gleaming iota after another.
we look at each other and
burst into laughter -
teleported back to being young.
always holding on to one
another, hues of pink and
purple.

the milk you spat all over me.
more laughter.
you shift next to me as the
clouds darken, all the screaming.
sisterhood comes with painful duality.
laughs coupled by yelling and then
laughing again.
our grip never loosens.
we're gonna make it, deal?

deal.

-Lulu Rodriguez

Sea Battle: Aftermath

We're not as still
as an aquarium
but suffocating on foam
and sand after a duel
with the ocean –

facedown, receiving the tail-end of the current, seismic quaking.

Water cannot fill us.
Sand stopped tasting like grains centuries ago.

Raw sea remains cause hallucinations –

maharajas receiving gifts –
demotion of old middle schools – galoshes lost weeks ago.

No guts or glory here,
just the spinning entirety
of the situation caterwauling
inside of our heads.

Follow the line
of glittering stones
to the reef
and fold right in.

-Samuel Strathman

Deciphering the Madness

The susurrus calling of the night as it slowly coils around the folds of my ears weaving a mystery every time I press my ears to this night with its black teeth, The days have peered long enough into my soul and came back empty-handed. I'm appalled by its loss every single time. I sit outside the quaint cafe at the end of my street and count the steps of every passerby, as they move past me. I am counting time through the hurried steps of this city. The city which reeks of the pain in the day, the city which weeps quietly at night. An invisible rush, a pied piper calling towards the shining beacon. Sometimes I think everyone is leaving this city as it empties its sorrows into the ocean, surrounding this city. Hanging to its sinews by numerous frail bridges connecting its entrails and muscles and bones to the body of the outside world. This exodus is nothing but a false sense of protection for those with hopes seeded in those bleary eyes that wake up every morning to become part of a hamster on the wheel routine, scuttling towards an end, which has no beginning. I take the next sip of my piping hot coffee as I count the hurried throbs of this city, the clickety clickety syncopated rhythm and deep inside I know there is a method to this madness I so fervently try to decipher every damn morning.

-Megha Sood

The Broken Carousel

Draped in the silence of the night
is the silhouette of a horse
wrapped under the layers of that canopy
covered in the layers of dust and grime
in the middle of the square

An extravaganza
a majestic sight for everyone to cherish and see
a fanfare for everyone to dwell in
to relinquish their broken dreams and
crestfallen hopes

For a moment of that turn
that swirl,
on its majestic back
like the serenity of the swirling dervish
seeking that moment of union with the divine

They came rushing for it
for the cost of a dime
that magical land you are swept into
for the brief moment of time
is now standing still
like a locked gaze in time.

-Megha Sood

La primera vez que vi la luz

Tomé consciencia de un latir desbocado,
localizado ahí adentro, en mi hipocentro.
Algo me resbalaba por las venas, por los ojos, por el alma; un líquido
incandescente, una suerte de hechizo.

Pude verlo todo por un momento:
las caricias estables, las heridas punzantes,
el éxtasis fugaz, el llanto inoportuno.
Y yo, en mi ignorancia, añoré todo aquello.

Sucumbí ante las terribles maravillas.
Entregué mi paz por una probabilidad furtiva,
por las promesas de un creador imprudente.

La atmósfera comenzó a crujir, a tambalearse.
Comencé a hundirme en un fango invisible
y en el fondo se secó mi consciencia brevemente.

La incertidumbre se esparció entre mis entrañas.
Aún no había nadie y, sin embargo, presentí mi destino.
Creí escuchar las risas amargas, el llanto eléctrico.

El tiempo comenzaba a partirse en instantes.
Miré hacia arriba en donde un vórtice se abría, alejando a la oscuridad
con apatía

Cerré los ojos mientras me arrepentía
y de pronto fui absorbido en un estallido psicótico.
Sentía que me ahogaba, que me deshacía.

Intenté morir y sin querer mis párpados se separaron.
Ahí se apareció por vez primera: pálida, gloriosa,
iluminando ese vacío repleto de melancolía
que pronto comencé a llamar existencia.

Y lloré.

-Ruben Pineda

The First Time I Saw Light

I became aware of an unbounded heartbeat,
I felt it between my entrails, down in my hypocenter.
Something was sliding through my veins, through my eyes, through
my soul;
An incandescent liquid, some sort of sorcery.

I could see everything for a moment:
The stable caresses, the stabbing wounds,
The fleeting ecstasy, the inopportune weeping.
And I, lost in my ignorance, longed for everything.

I succumbed to those terrible delights,
I surrendered my peace to a furtive probability,
 To the promises of a reckless creator.

The atmosphere began to crumble, to stagger.
And I sunk into an invisible mud.
At the bottom my consciousness dried briefly.

The uncertainty spread through my insides.
There was no one yet, nevertheless, I sensed my fate.
I thought I heard bitter laughter, electric crying.

Time was beginning to break into instants.
 I looked up where a vortex was opening,
Driving away the darkness with apathy.

I closed my eyes while I regretted everything,
And suddenly I was absorbed in a psychotic shattering.

I felt I was drowning, I felt I was melting.

I tried to die and my eyelids opened by accident.
There she was, for the first time: pale, glorious,
Lighting up this melancholy-filled emptiness
 that I soon began to call existence.

And then I cried.

-Ruben Pineda

Taxidermia infinita

Afuera la lluvia destroza el pavimento,
los charcos empapan a los ancianos
y los niños piensan que son impermeables.

Aquí dentro la tormenta empezó antes, en
algún momento entre el diluvio y Noé
 y el anuncio de mi boda de papel.

Somnoliento, estoy sumido en mi silla giratoria,
todo lo que miro, me agarra y me interroga, mas
todo me es extraño: la voz en mi garganta,
el aire entre mis uñas, la sangre en mi memoria.

Mis pies están húmedos, la madera reblandecida,
epistaxis de mis ojos, la causa establecida.
Y las gotas caen, como caen los meses y las torres.

Me mantendré condenado e impasible,
inmerso en una taxidermia infinita,
mientras la lluvia no pare, mientras la lluvia sea mía.

-Ruben Pineda

Infinite Taxidermy

Outside, the rain is wrecking the pavement,
The puddles soak the elderly,
And the children think they´re impervious.

Here, inside, the storm began earlier,
In a moment between Noah and the Flood
And the announcement of my paper wedding.

Drowsy, I am sunken into my swivel chair,
And everything I look at, grabs me and interrogates me,
But everything is strange to me: the voice in my throat,
The air between my nails, the blood in my memory.

My feet are wet, the wood is softened,
Epistaxis from my eyes, the established cause.
And the drops fall, like the months, like the towers.

I will keep myself damned and impassible,
Immersed in an infinite taxidermy,
While the rain continues, while the rain belongs to me.

-Ruben Pineda

De plata y dunas

Qué delicado puede ser el minuto
si se rompe
entre manos vacías.
Dime qué escurre
sino ausencias consagradas al estío.
Dime a quién llevas a cuestas
sin descubrir al ocaso que sangra
y cuando se vuelve
eres tú
mi soledad compartida
desprendiendo llanto
al filo del día.

Hemos crecido en nostalgia
y nos hemos adaptado
a la dulzura de la palabra que acaricia
cada noche
cuando el minuto es nuestro
y no lo compartimos con nadie
porque en cada segundo te veo
y todos los sueños se enhebran
en un verso.
Podemos ver el mar que se hinca
como un eunuco
al costado del amor
y a la sombra de la luna
que nos habla
danzando sobre su hermosa superficie
de plata, y dunas.

-Maritza Sara Luza Castillo

Of Silver and Dunes

How delicate a minute can be
If it breaks
In empty hands.
Tell me what runs out
If not absences devoted to summer.
Tell me whom you carry on your back
Without realizing at sunset that he is bleeding,
 And when he turns around
It is yourself,
My shared loneliness,
Releasing sadness
All day long.

We have grown up with nostalgia
And we have adapted
To the sweetness of words that caress.
 Each night,
When the minute is ours,
And we don't share it with anyone,
Because in each second I see you,
And all dreams are tangled
In a verse.
We can see the ocean genuflecting
Like a eunuch,
 Side by side with love,
In the shadow of the moon
That speaks to us,
Dancing on its beautiful surface
 of silver, and dunes.

-Maritza Sara Luza Castillo

Mint Tea and Mini Skirts

I carry these secrets like an infection of the mouth. My truths chapping and tearing at my lips, and words may be the remedy but I don't let them out. Instead there are blood stains where my smile should be. Biting back dry confessions.

I'm sorry, I don't mean to be distant.

Forgive me for ignoring your constant calls.

I know that you care. About my health and well being.

And I have been avoiding you.

I have.

I suppose that I'm afraid. Terrified.

But every time you mention my cells or their abnormality or another necessary test or procedure or treatment...

I shake and crumble under the weight.

Because, and forgive me, but I'm afraid.

I don't want to die.

I remember

She stood there, calmly, looking at me with concerned eyes, waiting for my response. At the time I could think only of the refreshing sweetness of sugar crystals buried within the body of a ripened watermelon. And a world that produces such succulence as this cannot, I reason, birth something as treacherous as cancer.

"No, doctor," I say at last, "I don't have any questions."

There are words living in my throat, crawling and scratching, trying to escape. But I gulp and swallow them down. I keep my cheeks sucked in. I hold my breath. I furrow my brows in an internal struggle against my tongue. But sometimes I forget. I let my guard down. And I un grit my teeth.

And a cashier casually asks, "how are you today?"

And I projectile vomit on her the word poison that has been gagging me. "I am ok, I guess," I respond, "But my doctor keeps repeatedly quoting cancer. So maybe I'm not."

-Ali Blanco

If I Am Reborn

I prune and deadhead my plants with care
And I am sure they will flower more beautifully than before.
I know that I need to cut behaviours that no longer serve me
Trim many toxic traits from my personality.
I want to bloom more brilliantly
But I am afraid,
I've spent so long watering weeds.
What will remain after the withered is cleared away?

I have a talent
For maintaining appearances
Happy is my alter ego and every so often she is allowed to come out to play.
Laughter is a neighbour who comes to call every other Thursday between 5-8
I am a talented illusionist
I put on these parties so effortlessly, it would seem they were there always.
I Trick myself into thinking that my table has ever been set for more than one.
14 seconds after I kiss you goodbye and walk you to the door, I hang my demeanour to dry.
House empty, I pretend no more
I don't tell you that before today I hadn't spoken to another human in eight days
I didn't tell you that the last 8 days blended with the last 48.
But I have the skill of kissing with passion
And I guess that's all you need to know.

If I am reborn
Gifted with a clean slate,
Will I make the same mistakes?
Can I follow the light?
Or Will I awaken still in darkness, thirsting for pain?

-Ali Blanco

Like Leaves

I am the last leaf to fall
Falling out and away from normal and reason.
Falling toward you
In love, in season.
Swaying freely in the breeze,
Dancing in the wind with death.

My first love was autumn
Leaves are most beautiful in their death.
Lively greens become violet and maroon.
Brilliant shades of fire.
Decorating the ground around home tree with their bodies.
Laid to rest like flowers at a grave.
Are we thus perfected in our passing?
Or does knowledge and fear of demise cast pale,
grey shadow upon our cheeks? The leaf embraces its end.

A Sacrificial act for the good of mother tree,
Plunging downward so that tree may survive.
Leaves carried in the breeze
Gathering and Rustling and singing
Dancing in the wind with death.
Let me sway to sleep like a leaf,
Drifting without regret towards my end Coloured like the sunset.
Like the sunset on fire.
Let me be an image which inspires poetry.

-Ali Blanco

Our Streets are Tarred with Candle Wax

and littered with a number of half burnt
candles, left at the mercy of the night wind –

howling and rambling like the voice of
protesters, like the lament of a mother

as she's been taken away from the log
of her child's body, like the silent screams

of innocent bodies emptied into the river
behind Awkuzu SARS.

These candles burn for the dreams stopped
halfway and configured into nightmares,

for beds lying empty in cold rooms,
for clothes stuffed in sacs begging

for the warmth of their owner's body.
These candles burn for the sun

that sets at noon, for innocent eyes closed up
by the sharp blaze of police bullets,

for blood drying up by the roadside,
for the unheard sobs of a father digging

to bury his daughter. These candles
burn for the tears of a mother whose

wrapper is damped by an ocean of
consolation over her wasted son,

they burn for a land where to run into
the police station is to become a dog

that escapes the hyena and
limps into the den of jackals.

Our streets are tarred with our brothers'
blood and littered with the bullets of cops.

-Taofeek Ayeyemi (Aswagaawy)

------

*SARS is an acronym for Special Anti-Robbery Squad, a now defunct
unit of Nigeria Police Force following a nationwide protest calling the
government to #EndSARS and #EndPoliceBrutality

Sòrò Sókè and Break the Long Chain of Oppression

Sòrò sókè and let the world hear you
describe the thickness of your blistered soles.

Sòrò sókè so the chain of brutality and
repression may rattle into silence;

No dey disguise that your stars are aligned
when there are a million faults in them.

Sòrò sókè and be pulled out of your
shell of complacency and cowardice;

Do not wait until police bullets tear your skin
before understanding the plight of protesters,

because no be beans to leave the comfort
of one's room and pour oneself into the street:

to raise the placards under the scorching sun or the pelting rain;
to risk being laid by the waywardness of stray bullets.

Sòrò sókè because whether you speak
or not, you're not safe from the SARS' grip,

For there's no suspect in their law:
in the eyes of one with a hammer, everything is a nail.

-Taofeek Ayeyemi (Aswagaawy)

•Ṣọ̀rọ̀ sókè is Nigerian Yoruba slang meaning "speak up." No dey disguise is Nigeria pidgin meaning "do not disguise" asking one to firmly maintain his position. No be beans is Nigerian pidgin meaning "it's not easy." SARS is Special Anti-Robbery Squad which was called to be prescribed through the #EndSARS Protest due to their abuse of power.

October 20, 2020

Home is where we run to when the world
flogs us; but in this home, everybody is running away.

For here is where you protest against brutality
and your placards are lowered with strikes of cruelty.

At Lekki, we didn't know savagery was being cooked
when the security cameras were removed

and the lights were put off, until when bullets
started flying, guns singing the alliteration 20-2020

while protesters choreograph into oblivion.
The only weapons the protesters were carrying

were the Green White Green flags,
their only war song was the National anthem.

Since Green RED Green would've saved them
from the soldiers' bullets, it is what I say now

when asked the colour of my country's flag.
Home is where we run to when the world flogs us,
and some mothers are home waiting for children
that will never return, fallen while asking for a better home.

-Taofeek Ayeyemi (Aswagaawy)

Headstone

We are asked to peel potatoes.
We are told to put the skins,
which my sister can produce in a single
spiral strip, into a dented metal bowl
between us.

We will save them for soup.
I do not think the popular thing is true;
death is not "just a part of life."
My sister finishes flaying her spuds, bounds off
into the unmowed yard.

It is harder than that;
It is not as if life and death amicably separated
like an out-of-love couple so that they may find
more satisfying companions.

Dad reaches inside for breath enough to call his youngest back
but she's off into the hay, the tresses of what's left of the day's light,
blonde like Mom was even up to this day last year.
My sister will not remember. I will not outlive my grief.
When Mom laughed, she laughed from her soul, they said.

I remember it like that now, growing in a room
like the steam from her scrumptious kitchen magic.
I will not outlive my grief.
But maybe it is not impossible to live;
extremes can exist back-to-back.

I give you the zebra, I give you sunset, I give you a naked potato
clutched in accidentally sliced fingers. Dad is still looking into where
his girl disappeared, past it now, to the yard of stones
displaying summaries of entire lives. Death is apart from life, he whispers,
grazing the pane with his fingertips. It will always be as hard as that.

-Megan Wildhood

A Divorce Decree

My marriage was a mirage.
the way wood chips mirage a forest:

you think there's something real there.
You think, *wood is softer than concrete*

so if I fall, ah, what the hell? You keep
playing even though you are alone

and every other relationship you see
is between adults who catch each other.

Actually, that's exactly right:
wood chips are dead forest

that are soft (as in, not strong)
and smell living. But they are dead.

Okay, so it's not actually exact.
My marriage was never living.

Only dead. Only dead.

The day the final orders were filed
and put on public record

for all to see my failure - I didn't
even get the dignity of real dead-tree

paper because even the law has caught up
and is virtual now -

I did a happy dance while sobbing.
First time in my life I've done *that*.

I cried like I had just been born.
And that is exactly right: I had.

-Megan Wildhood

Storm Cellar—1948

When night storms
brought danger, Grandma
led us into the 'fraidy hole.'

Down there scorpions ruled.
Centipedes crawled
down collars.
Dank things squiggled
across our arms.

Forgetting the beast outside,
we huddled around
our lantern like cavemen
at the dawn of creation,
afraid to move.

Later, when the storm had
passed, I went to sleep
and dreamed of clouds
with stinging tails.

-LaVern Spencer McCarthy

Ants in The Sugar Bowl

Miles of black ants have
come to steal from my
porcelain sugar bowl.
Each grabs a grain, scurries
away into unknown realms.

They thieve for their queen, no doubt.
When she sees those sweet diamonds,
I'll bet she rolls in them,
stuffs herself, sports them as
antennae bracelets, emits
ant cackles of pure satisfaction.

She is unaware that I could
eliminate her minions in
seconds, but I only watch
the mindless toil, meditate on
the grand scheme of things. Who
am I to deny them their purpose?

-LaVern Spencer McCarthy

I satisfy the muse —

— my songwriter of love of death lilies and earth soil
he walks out of me lands on the sheets scattered
pages strewn across the floor demands attention when

words muddle when I refuse the reach
muddle when my heart and my swollen angel
refuse the beating

life's yellow canaries caught in the jaws
feathers transparent at the edges fleeting

those black curls and twisted backs that
swirl their bodies like salivating cats
circling the ankles waiting to be served or

men in single file who know that look in the eyes
recognize the ripe tone of skin flushed
the dewdrops that escape from the edges of lips and
breasts that lift that demand attention

my flesh manipulates this muse calms his greedy tongue
with these words I find daunting words I craft
to soothe to sing out those tired fantasies of mermaids
stranded on rocks their pink mouths unhinged salivating
waiting to be served to be saved

oh those lullabies of lies that puff his chest with strokes of
undulating love notes flagrantly loosen from my throat
from my fingertips

I place his prize on the platter at the edge of his table
like robusto cigars with heavy scented tobacco
soft notes of earth sweet spice I
pour his whiskey into the beveled crystal

He is
 —so easily satisfied

-Jen Yáñez-Alaniz

Each of Them Turns Away

That night at the Amp Room,
dimmed lights, poetry revving in the background,
never could decide if I like open mics, but there we were again.
We laughed, drank a bit too much vodka, doodled on our palms,
even wrote poetry.

We pretended the altar at the church wasn't ours,
abandoned our prayers for a bit.
Let the darkness and raw poetic verses
reach us from the stage.
We talked about this god of ours
and his angels. How we were positive
we were sitting on wings, keeping them from flight.

But we love our angels held captive, love the nod
they get from our god, mostly because they have given up on us;
all of them — god — the angels — our spouses.
Each of them turns away.
They know to let us burden ourselves with guilt,
our inability to forgive, to let verses from the poets
sit thick on our chests.
But everyone knows we go home after the poets have
toasted the last call, after the poetry has ended,
	and the altar at the church
calls us back home.

-Jen Yáñez-Alaniz

En tus manos

Borra de mis labios
el necio sabor de los tuyos.
Arranca de mi piel
las huellas de sal
que son fuego entre el fuego
e incineran el alma
bajo
el lluvioso cielo de julio.
Ven
pero no me abraces.
Me ha asqueado el ser cautivo
que subyace
tras la orfandad de esos ojos
entrenados
para esconder serpientes.
Si quieres hablar, ven.
Acércate de espaldas
y empuja aquella verdad que siempre te dio la cara
sobre vestigios falsos de ternura. Néctar ilusorio el cual bebí,
hasta la última gota,
embriagando todo el tiempo
tu genuino demonio
reflejado en el espejo.
Ahora el jazmín duerme
y escurre lentamente
el agua que tú prodigaste
con un pseudónimo de ti mismo. Ven te digo.
y no arrojes más tierra
sobre el cuerpo que en tus manos
ha fallecido.

-Maritza Sara Luza Castillo

we're
all in
this
together

In Your Hands

Erase from my lips
The ludicrous taste of yours.
Rip off from my skin
The traces of salt,
The fire among fires
That burns my soul
Under
The rainy July sky.
Come here,
But do not embrace me.
Your captive being
Disgusts me,
Behind those orphaned eyes
Trained
To hide serpents.
If you want to talk, come here.
Walk backward toward me
Pushing along this truth
That has always faced you
Above the fake remains of tenderness.
I drank that fictitious nectar
Down to the last drop,
A nectar that always intoxicated
Your true demon
Reflected in the mirror.
Now the jasmine is asleep.
And the water you squandered
 Under a pseudonym of yourself
Trickles down slowly.

Come here, I say.
And don't toss more dirt
On a body that has died
In your hands.

-Maritza Sara Luza Castillo

Nocturno

Ilusorio recorte de días
sobre delgadas pupilas
 del espejo o la ventana

en la calle la oscuridad
desnuda llaves que tocan
en el corazón de cada puerta
 pero nadie abre

cierra el candado de la noche
 su insomne celda…

-Darío Oliva

Puzle

Puzle
encastrar las sombras
y los huesos   en el césped
hasta que el recuerdo
recomponga soledades
descalzas y de espalda contra espalda
en silencioso
vaivén de sol y aguas

esperar que su boca
remonte barriletes   mariposas
y el aguijón de avispa de sus ojos
no se hunda en la luz para eclipsarla…

No me dejó respuestas
 sólo preguntas
y este faltante de una pieza
que su inconstante corazón
                ya no completa.

-Darío Oliva

I

Es peor negarlo todo
                              no querer o no saber
engañarse o desdoblarse
Esta especie de liturgia o absurda ciclotimia
en que muere la evidencia y se tapan las pupilas
Habrá que mirar otra vez
ver belleza en la polilla que se apila en el asfalto
(no) mirar para otro lado
Ver el verde de otros tiempos en el tizne del presente
de estos campos calcinados
No quiero vivir del pasado
ni vivir siendo el culpable de seguir alimentando
esta fauna gris de insectos
No me gusta esta manera
esta forma de insistencia de abusar del palimpsesto
donde siempre en la hoja en blanco
queda el poso de otro escrito
Es mejor querer la muerte
                              las arrugas los gusanos
la funesta consecuencia de esperar lo que nos venga
la conciencia polvorienta de que somos parte activa
de esta arena circundante
el desierto movedizo por detrás y por delante
al que ahora regresamos
Abrazarnos a la muerte a la hora de caer
ser más lúcidos que nunca
más ingrávidos que nunca
porque siempre es más virtuoso el visible menoscabo
de aceptar la decadencia que mirar para otro lado
y vivir siempre del loto

-Pedro López Fernández

II

El olvido nos deshace aunque aún estemos vivos
Es de noche y en lo oscuro cuesta mucho ver las flores
el dolor la desmemoria
la manera nebulosa de expoliarnos el pasado
Hay un daño en todo esto que nos ancla sobre el rostro
este impulso de llorar
Nos consuela de momento comprobar que no hay espejos
ni siquiera un charco artero que conserve entre sus aguas
las facciones de esta cara
o el guiño en el paisaje del destello de estos ojos
No hay tampoco nada en esto que nos hable de tristeza
la manera silenciosa de sentarnos en la orilla mientras vemos
todo el tiempo a los ríos escaparse
ese modo sin tocarse en que el agua y nuestras manos
se entrelazan por los dedos
Es posible realmente que en el fondo de este asunto
haya un ciclo natural
un mojarnos cuando llueve porque el agua es lo que tiene
y que así funciona esto
Y la vida también tiene que a veces se llega
a ese punto donde empieza la caída

Y caer también es vida pintar una equis con tiza una equis sobre el pecho
donde intrínseca a la herida luce más la cicatriz Porque tampoco es funesto ni absurdo
anhelarse en ese punto de querer ya no estar vivo salvo quizás ese espacio intermedio
entre el punto de haber muerto
y el olvido del espejo

-Pedro López Fernández

Pacto

sin pautas morales
 sin cordura
golpe de cuerpos
 de intimidades
esbozadas
 en lienzo de soledad
ajenos al mundo
con tan poco
con tanto de nada
en simples grafitis de palabras
permanecemos

-SAHILÍ CRISTIÁ LARA

Amiga

Amiga;
aquí te espero
en el mediodía salvaje de las flores; cuando tus ojos ardían como dos
fogatas yo orinaba borracho en las calles
y bebía los últimos sorbos de un vaso de vino.

Tan larga fue la noche…
como la muerte en que nos conocimos que me parecen eternas las vere-
das que alguna vez recorrimos juntos.

Si te dijera que no creo en el amor…
        me creerías?

Te he hablado en sueños,
en mi lenguaje de conjuros…
prometiste no dejarme nunca
mientras mis palabras te guiñaban los ojos
 y tu nombre aprendían de memoria.

Amiga;
desde aquí te ofrezco mi poesía
como un río agonizante
que se hace camino hasta ti…

Sabes;
eres parte de mi alma y te pertenezco.
Por ahora me conformo
con mirarte siempre de lejos,
orinando borracho en las calles

bebiendo los últimos sorbos
        de un vaso de vino…
 esperándote siempre
en el mediodía salvaje de las flores.

-Nelson Eric Castillo inostroza

En el oscuro pueblo de los rieles oxidados

Al fin todo tiene sentido...
tragaré tus recuerdos con un par de cervezas
 en el oscuro pueblo de los rieles oxidados.
Con un puñado de gramos en la pipa
me sentaré a ver cómo se desangran
          mis palabras
en un lento vaivén hasta perder la memoria.

A ella no le importa que te ame.
Descubrí un día lo absurdo que es
 no pertenecer a lugar alguno
en el oscuro pueblo de los rieles oxidados.

A ella no le importa que te ame,
ni que pase todo el día pensando en ti…

A ella le da lo mismo quedar así, vacía.

—No tengas miedo —me dijo un día—.
A veces la vida no es como esperabas,
pero ten por seguro que algún día serás feliz.

Ahora que lo pienso un poco,
          al fin todo tiene sentido…
ella sí que sabía mentir.

—No tengas miedo —me dijo un día
en el oscuro pueblo de los rieles oxidados.

-Nelson Eric Castillo inostroza

Cape Point

There is blasphemy in gazing
off this cliff
where the diligent tides that plaster nature's walls
have hurriedly smeared
the clay of colors on the fierce rockface
and fled;
and the terrified gulls forget that they can fly
and tumble
to the mercy of the slapping wind; all
made rags by confusion.
We dare to look
only because love gives us backbone
and only that, because,
caught between currents,
we do not have the time for fear.
Heavy mountains tremble
beneath the salty sky,
against the spinning gusts,
and we alone can
glimpse
the secret dotted line splitting the oceans
and, from here, go treading
on a journey no weather-hardened fisherman
could ever boat.
Like the sudden prayer
the birds utter to the crags
becomes a squawk,
like petals shuddering from
the steely touch of snowdrops,

or a gorgeous woman steadily going insane,
intensity sours immediately.
Come and live with me in another country.

-Stuart Stromin

I have to know the wage of text

For a poet, silence is an acceptable, even flattering response,
claimed Sidonie-Gabrielle Colette.

Another claimed
that the calm that is the history of silence
is the poet's revenge.

Look, I walk around with a quill
between my teeth

Some people have their sensory hearing absorbed into in the most un-
expected organs, and some will qualify in silence, accordingly I have to
know the wage
of
text —

Surely, the initial reaction in humans
in their early lives is the voice, after
which everything else is a charade.

עֲלַי לָדַעַת אֶת שְׂכַר הַמִּלָּה
רֶבַע מְשׂוֹרֵר, שְׁתִיקָה הִיא תְּגוּבָה קְבִילָה, אֲפִילוּ מַחְמִיאָה,
טָעֲנָה סִידוֹנִי גַבְרִיאֵל קוֹלֶט.

אַחֵר טָעַן
שֶׁהַדְּמָמָה שֶׁהִיא הַהִיסְטוֹרְיָה שֶׁל הַשְּׁתִיקָה
הִיא נִקְמָתוֹ שֶׁל הַמְשׂוֹרֵר.

רְאִי, אֲנִי מִסְתּוֹבֶבֶת עַל עֵט קוּלְמוֹס
בֵּין הַשְּׁנַיִם

יֵשׁ אֲנָשִׁים שֶׁהַשְּׁמִיעָה הַחוּשִׁית שֶׁלָּהֶם נִקְלְטָה בְּאֵיבָרִים הֲכִי לֹא צְפוּיִים,
וַאֲחָדִים יַסְגּוּ יַסְגִּי בִּשְׁתִיקָה, לְפִיכָךְ. עָלַי לָדַעַת אֶת שְׂכָרוֹ
שֶׁל
— הַמֶּלֶל

אֵלֶּה, הַתְּגוּבָה הָרִאשׁוֹנִית אֵצֶל בְּנֵי אָדָם
בְּרֵאשִׁית שֶׁחַיֵּיהֶם, הִיא הַקּוֹל, לְ,
אַחַר מִכֵּן לָךְ שְׁאֵרָה הַזֶּה הַצָּגָה.

-Tali Cohen Shabtai

The Truth

You can always turn to
death
except for the dead themselves –

that's a purely rhetorical insight.

It's always possible to turn to sleep
and die in it
in an arbitrary unit of time
in a simulated
death –

It's also an insight in a man's
head.

About that it is said
that/
sleep is a great thing. Death is better than it. Not being born at all is a
miracle, of course.

From here, facing here or there
death
is static in its existence.

Arbitrary or
eternal that exists out of time.

That's how humans are!

ל תּוֹנַפְל רְשָׁפָא דיְמָת
תֶּנֶעַמ
פְּרַט לְמַתְיִס עֲצֶמָס-

זֹו תֻּבְנַה רֹטְרִית גְרִידָא.

הָנֵיש ל תּוֹנַפְל רְשָׁפָא גֵּג דיְמָת
ו לַמֹּוּת בָּק
בֹּיחְדָת זֶמָ נ שְׁרֹורְיֹתִית
בַּמֵיתָה
מְדֹומָה -

לֵש וֹשֹאּרְב הָנַבֻת גֵּג יהֹוז
אֶדָס.

עַל כְּדֶ נ אָמַר
/ש
שֵׁנַה איה רָבָּד הֶנֶדְר. מָעֲנֻת עָדִיף עֵלְיֶה, אל הֵיִּוֹנֻלְד כְלָל זֶהו נֶס, כְמַוֻבָן.

מְפַהֶ, פְּנֶיִס כַּל וֹאֹ לְכָאֹו
הַמַּעֲנֶת
הוא סְטַטֶי בַּקְיֻּמֹו.

שֶׁרְיֹורְתֶי אוֹ
נֶצְחִי ה קֵיּיָס-מַחֹוצ לַזמָן.

כָּכָה
זֶה בֶּנֶ אָדָס!

-**Tali Cohen Shabtai**

Dancing Tiles

Tile on the wall
tile next to tile
an emblem, a figure,
square dissecting polygon,
line penetrating circle,
a meaningful leaf,
pick a favourite
the blind will be led.
Old tile new tile
red on blue
sorrow over bliss
avenidas* crossing avenidas
cracked azulejos* of many pasts.
How can a fado
reverberate over shiny facades?
Tile waves cascading
seven lisboan hills
brown roof abyss
one-man balconies.
Hanging lanterns mirrored
on noiseless, elusive tuk-tuks*
instant images carried away
tied on lazy pigeon legs.
The ocean; the lighthouse; the bridge
all I could see
coração*
obrigado*
and a distant, vibrant lament
all I could hear -- all I could feel.

-**Christos R. Tsiailis**

*Avenida: avenue
*azulejos: glazed, ceramic tiles in different colours and designs on building facades everywhere in Lisbon.
*tuk tuk: small electric cars for city tours.
*coração: heart
*obrigado: thank you

Marsupial

The pouch is heavy
tells me the little one on the tree.
I see them as they flee
and turn my stare as hers
as fire tunes my instinct to a threatening, reddish roam.

silence for an eternal moment, and there I see.

No creature around really moves anymore.
No jumper jumps.
No devil dances and grunts.

I see their smiles condensed
condemned to eternal pity.

I see their palms firmly closed
and I see tails bending.

Can I hug you?
Asks the little one,
Can I hang on you, be a pouch for a while,
a grandfather to my own little one,
this thing without fur
that breathes the pink mist
from its tiny bloody nostrils?

Can I run?
I ask myself in disturbed tranquility, can I jump?
Can I carry something of my own at last?

We are out of the bush fires before I know,
but I rush back inside the smoke
jumping and growling
and I am forever more
-a marsupial-
for as long as my thick nostrils breathe.

-Christos R. Tsiailis

No Reason to Be Here

So far away, the cars can be
Seen only in one windowpane.
It is night, the thick night of winter
So thick I can't believe
the cars can even move
In their tiny frame.
They are going to places I used to love
To bars and restaurants, bookstores
home.
But the darkness caught up with me
It is thick, and I am hiding
In my empty office
As high as the freeway overpass
No work
No reason to be here
Eventually the sounds
of the building will scare me
And I will go home

-Don Webb

My Mother Bought This Table in 1958

Two SeaWorld of Texas glasses
faded after many dishwasher baptisms
celebrate cetacean slavery and death
on my late-night table.
My letters asking for catalogs.
A coffee can pressed into yeoman service
as a pencil and pen holder.
A brain which sees the yew rune
in yeoman.
The yew flame sputters.
It grows greendark in graveyards.
A phone book showing a girlchild
playing with a computer.
A box of my books for Mark.
A fan made from water buffalo hide
bought by Mom in Bangkok
in the floating market
for Christmas in Austin.
My wallet. A melmac sugar bowl.
Pizza bux. A rolodex. A roll of tape.
Three beer bottle openers in a toot.
A red stapler, Bostitch, of course.
My wife's keys. A bottle cap.
A telephone. A notebook for a novel.
An incomplete postcard. Air. The key
to my life.
This poem.

-Don Webb

Dancing in the ER

The beautiful day breaks the silence
of a foggy commute, scatters morning blues,
the dew I dance through, the blooming bluebonnets
where I quickly click smart-phone pics,
jiggle in bliss. Dancing brings bees
to the buzz and buzz to the bees.
If I am stung as I run away,
(which happens) and an allergic reaction
creates a spreading red bubble
that lands me in the packed ER,
I can entertain the overactive staff
long enough for them to stop
and watch me dancing.
The nagging itchiness caused by cut grass
I waded through to reach the bluebonnets,
the itch I can't stop scratching this reaction
again, guess what? I'll dance to help me
forget about it. In fact, let's convince
frontline workers, nurses to celebrate
the happy dance. Left arm, right arm, wave.
Hip bumping big booty shake. Left leg,
right leg, stomp-stomp-stomp. Step around,
grapevine down the line. Cheers to the freedom
to move, cheers to boogey nights, hand jive,
break-dancing moods. Oh, happy dance,
you bring joy to pandemic life.

-Laurie Kolp

Since Mom's No Longer Here

Cleaning up the mess, Dad and I finally work together:
he rinses plates, I place them in dishwasher. He says

we must handwash last dish—an old charred pan
with brisket drippings that we can't pour down the pipes.

I hold still in kitchen sink an empty soup can,
the perfect seal to catch accidental spills

from seeping down the drain. I watch Dad fill the can
with grease, my mind at ease within the moment.

I'm careful not to move my hand but thick liquid
trickles down my thumb, the tears I've shed for weeks.

My mouth an O as my eyes dart up to meet his
smile, his meaning clear, his words *I gotcha* treasured.

-Laurie Kolp

Beyond the Sloping Road

Dusk's silky cape of coral swirls
draping curls: the future
past the horizon,
a picture-perfect postcard set
before us.
Lovebugs hug the windshield
wipers, lovebugs
hanging on for dear life,
hanging on like us.
I want to jump from this convertible
and soar into the sorbet sunset,
scoop up the last bit
of lusciousness with you.
Everyone would call us
Superman and Lois Lane,
and we would strive to stay alive
in this world set before us
no matter how bleak it seemed.

-Laurie Kolp

The Foreignness of Forgiveness

In the Nahuatl to Spanish side of Molina's dictionary
we read: "Teyolia. el alma, o anima."
But, did we believe in a soul?
On the surface,
teyoliatl looks like a noun.
If we try to break it down
we get teyoli and atl,
ATL, water.
So we say "okay, it's some kind of water".

yoli looks like the verb
YOLi, to live.
So now we think
it must somehow
be related to aguas vivas,
and te must be TE,
someone, people.

But yoli cannot be
YOLi because
YOLi is intransitive
and cannot take,
the object TE.
We could say teyoli
is TEYOLiH,
the preterit
of TEYOLiA,
to make someone live.

But verbs are connected
to nouns by CA.
So we should expect
TEYOLiHCAATL
We're way off!

Besides,
life is YOLiZTLi.
Let's take a different approach.

What if it's not a noun?
What if it's a verb
disguised as a noun?
If we remove the noun marker
we're left with teyolia.
This looks like a
transitive verb YoLiA or YOLiA,
with the nonspecific
human object TE.
We haven't come
upon such a verb.
But there are many
i/iA verb pairs (aQUi/aQUiA,
OLINi/OLINiA,
iHUiNTi/iHUiNTiA, etc).

So, we could say
there might be a pair YOLi/YOLiA.
Then, TEYOLiA
would meen "it makes people live".
And, TEYOLiATL would be

the thing that makes people live.

That's not how
you nominalize verbs.
If there was a verb YOLiA,
we'd get 4 agentive nouns:
TEYOLiHQUi,
TEYOLiANi,
TEYOLIZQUi,
 and YOLIZTLi.
But not TEYOLiATL.

In the Spanish to Nahuatl
section of Molina's dictionary
we read: "Alma o anima.
teyolia,
teyolitia,
teanima."

teyolia would be TEYOLiA,
he/she makes people live.
But not even Molina has a verb YOLiA.

And don't even think
teyolia could be someone's YOLiA,
 'cause this would be TEYOLiAUH.
teyolitia is TEYOLITiA,
he/she makes people live.
YOLi has 2 causative forms:
YOLiLTiA
and YOLITiA.

But not YOLiA.

teanima is a
Spanish/Nahuatl hybrid.
It'd meen someone's soul.
The use of Spanish anima
indicates this is a foreign concept.

The frailes used Spanhuatl
for foreign things.
Like pearl quauitl,
pear tree;
hicox, fig;
tiox, god;
angelotin, angels;
colos, cross; etc.

All the early grammarians were frailes.
That's why we find
alma, confesión, pecado,
fiesta de guardar,
bautismo, salvación, dios, etc.

We have to consider
that some terms
may have been
coined to answer
como se dice
esto o aquello.

Simeon also has teyoliatl.

But he based his dictionary
on Molina's.

Bierhorst doesn't have it.
Which means
it's not used in the Cantares.
Karttunen doesn't have it either.
Which means
she couldn't make sense of it.

"Ex Nihilo" -- out of nowhere
It seems,
at least to us,
that teyoliatl
is a word invented
to name something
the friars were describing.
The foreignness
of the concept
is reflected
in its ungrammatical
construction.

Special thanks to
From Ruben Ramirez "Huitzilmazatzin"

-Tezozomoc

Solastalgia

for Meda DeWitt and Nicole Masters

It has to be more
than a neologism.
More than an emotional
or an existential distress.

It has to be more
than the lived experience.
More than the negatively
perceived environmental change.

It has to be more
than the loss of 98%
of your land base.
More than 30 Million
whose trail of tears
walked onto the milky way;
the skyward roadway to the ancestors.

It has to be more
than the boarding-school-childish tears
as they flay your culture like a skin.
More than the
animalization at the hands of your oppressor.

It has to be more
than the fog of mourning.
More than what is
intransitively already lost.

It has to be more
than the homesickness
of post-traumatic stress.
More than the anxiety
of what is to be lost;
a kind of pre-traumatic stress.

It has to be more
than the volcanic eruptions.
More than the
destructive strip mining.

It has to be more than
the quotidian homesickness.
More than the distress
caused by social change.

Beyond the persistent
droughts of rural new South Wales.
Beyond the impact
of large-scale open-cut
wounds of coal mining
in the Upper Hunter Valley.

Beyond the loss of the
once predictable environment
in BIPOC communities.
Beyond the interaction
of society and community
social-political ways;
the experience of community
and its loss of power

over its well-being;
the potent impotency.

Beyond BIPOC communities
grounded in livelihoods tied
to the earth and the weather;
agrarians, fisher folks, and gatherers.

But the higher-income communities
can quickly rebuild their homes
after the destruction from a wild-fire;
wealth can shield you from that anxiety.

But wealth prevents
your community from mountaintop removal;
the toxic battery plant next to your golf course;
the political power that
wealth buys is preventive.

The lingering influence of interpersonal
violence, community conflict, family structures;
economic status will determine
the mental health and well-being.

The chain of causation
will show its slippage
with psycho-social distress
of emergency workers and
first responders due
to social community health deterioration;
putting them in post-traumatic
stress disorder,

depression,
and panic.

But we must move beyond
the historical traumas,
the intergenerational traumas,
and persistent external and self
inflicted stresses;
of social, economical, institutional,
judicial, and interpersonal.

We must move beyond the stress;
of prolonged exposure to physical,
mental, and spiritual oppression.

We must not suffer these epigenetic changes
to our progeny and lineage.
These ghosts haunting future generations;
who are not sure why
These afflictions are affecting them in known and unknown ways.

Ultimately, we are 8% originated from viruses,
more bacterial cells than human cells;
mycelial and evolutionary.

And finally, our quorum sensing
can be triggered by
Geosmin, the "odor of the earth"
at 5 parts per trillion.

-Tezozomoc

American Dream

There are dreams, we are sold
a sleepless life that we are told
is the epitome of what we are to reach for

in order to live the life we bleed for
handed to us before we even know we want it
based on imaginings of those who create for profit

Each day we lose a bit more of ourselves
to this empty shell of plaster, a well
surrounded by a white picket fence
that isn't made of wood, instead dense
with the dreams we once held as freedom
plastic, poly vinyl stakes pierced deep down

within

dreams

once believed in

Bodies fed by food not fit for consumption
Minds left to devices…not their own function

Spirits depleted of joy by demands of filling spaces

With materials flashing by so fast they leave no traces

Of what they were meant to do – make one whole

Instead of making things better for where it begins... the true soul
Fabrications created to keep control in check
Freedoms exchanged for mortal coils around our necks
Before our very eyes
fed are we these lies
accepted as truths
through digital feeding tubes

diluting

dreams

once believed in

Forced to live beyond means in our hands
false sense of security inflated by card scans
basic must haves become luxuries difficult to keep track
of what is needed versus what will maintain us dumb and slack
eyes glassy, shoulders slumped under the weight
of living … no … existing until the slate from the ground is staked

Boxed in to keep souls further out of touch from each other
Boxes telling us what to think before we know what thoughts to foster

Taking social exchange out of basic human touch
Leaving all suspicious of those even closest to us

We left our freedom at the door willingly
When the possibility of fear became reality

Darkening

Dreams

Once alight from within

For an enlightened society so bent on knowing everything
We know little or nothing of ourselves … lost tribes of queens and kings
Revolution begins not with the nameless enemies we're trained to fear

It starts with conquering the fear of within, making that pervasive fog clear
Reignite those burned dreams we're conditioned to put aside
By someone else's determination of what dreams should fill our minds

We need to awaken from this Sleepless dream
Of possessions that will outlast us and mean …

… Nothing

Of fears of one another for simply not knowing anything
Of hiding from truth, we know as self-evident

Awaken

Dreams

make them the new American Reality

-RescuePoetix

Una voz

In a celebration of life we sing and dance
Porque somos una voz

When injustice strikes our motherland
Nuestra gente in the middle of a long ignored fight
We raise our voices in unity
To strengthen the borinqueño in our blood

Being Puerto rican isn't a state of mind
Puerto rican is life blood – the single
flow through a heart that beats with rhythms
of el guiro, las congas el requinto
in time of Bomba y plena

With every breath we take our Puerto Rico back
We claim our independence from the slavery
Of outmoded thought and laws
That serve no one but the wealthy

Porque somos una voz
Hablamos la idoma de nuestra sangre
Our collective voice will be heard
Con una fuerza tan inmensa que nadie lo para
Nadie

Con nuestra propio fuego
Liberando lo nuestro
Con una voz

Aqui estamos presente
En una voz
Cantando de la isla del encanto
De la Estrella del Caribe

-RescuePoetix

Inheritance

Inheritance is an expectation of blood
that has long run thin
losing its strength through
generation
and generation
of diluted rebellions

until you don't even ask

why the pernil is cut before you put it in the mojo,

why the pasteles are made
the day after thanksgiving
in a marathon of papel and twine,

mounds of masa and achiote

why the olives are green
and
fingertips blackened
by the labor of love
that lost its meaning long ago

broken accents of tíos y tías
into the flat New Jersey
Puerto Rican Nasal correction
from children

who are taught

that brown skin is
a second class punishment

but not taught to love that skin and
the pain
sacrifice
laughter
rhythms with it

Inheritance
of blood
belief
change
trauma

passed down
from mother and father

meaning lotus flower
with the strength of Egyptian queens

Treated as a delicate Lilly
a rose whose petals fall in the heat

Underestimated and invisible
in the weeds of males

The melanin that was once my inheritance
thinned by the blood of savages
in the guise of men

Yet,
there was always hope
fierce determination to grow
beyond the boundaries
and limitations
of the five letters
expected to define
or wipe away
a heritage of blood

seen through the ideals of others

Along with the accent that should have rightfully been mine

The whole pernil
marinated and cooked slow and long
leaving that lingering hope of what's to come

It's taken one generation forward
To remind two generations back
That what's in a made-up name
is but a sound

Passed on through the divinity of ancestors

Clamoring to be remembered

In the pale skin stretched over the conga

Through the guiro's hollow screeches

Traditions of masa y achiote
deep into the night

Wrapped in hojas de plátano
Tied with butcher's twine

strong enough to keep secrets in
while the color bleeds out

-RescuePoetix

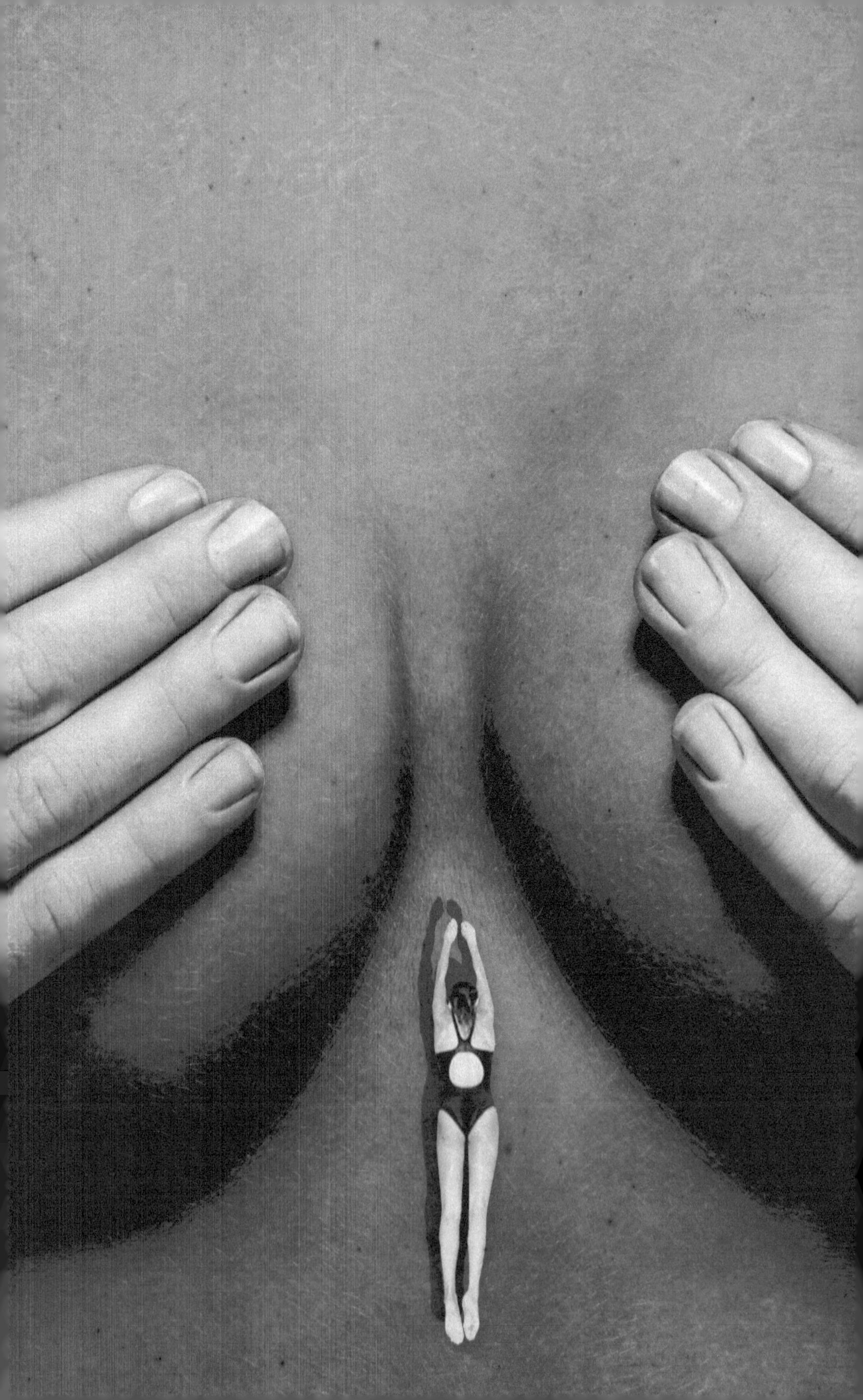

Cristalizar la soledad de una vida en la ciudad

Consumir la nostalgia
en los espacios vacíos
rostros amargos de semblante triste.

Todo lo construido
carece de Dios.
Todo lo que se destruye
es el principio del amor,

nadando sobre las ruinas,
descartando la mirada
dentro del alma
que no puede susurrar.
¿Dónde está la derrota?
En la cara de la ciudad
la prostituta, el obrero y el
transexual, los drogadictos que
saltan sobre los tejados,
buscando el sentido de su vida
 consumiendo el éxtasis
agotando la posibilidad,

recitando en los baños
sus absurdos poemas,
 rezando
llorando
insultando
abortando

descartan en cestas vacías
 sus fetos irreconocibles
feministas comunistas y adictos al speed.

Dentro de nosotros no hay
nada como la habitación del hotel antes
 de llegar,
incluso con nosotros dentro.

-Mahadma Solís

El fin de la comedia humana

Lo que realmente nos duele de la
tragedia es
que no estuvimos ahí.
En el incendio lo único que sobrevivió
fue la fotografía
que ella tomó el día de su boda.

En el cielo azul, un avión
en el mar, tu cuerpo flotando
el cuerpo que se desploma en el
asfalto dejando muestra
de su anatomía.

La corrupción del tiempo.

Lo que realmente te duele
 es
que cuando ella se despidió
el día del divorcio
te devolvió el anillo.

Duele que no estuviste ese día
el día que naciste
el día que mueras.

Dices que no te importa
dices que está todo bien
pero tiemblas de miedo.

Una pequeña explosión
dentro de ti,
la felicidad de estar cuando tu hija
nació escuchar su llanto por primera
 vez

sentir su cabello en tu brazo
descansar y saber, que esto también
te lo vas a perder.

Sabes que te lo vas a perder.

-Rosa Mendoza-Valencia

Elegía para un padre muerto

Es julio y amaneció lloviendo.
Lluvia mansa que acaricia el rostro,
suena en los tejados
como aleteo de golondrinas
y despierta un dolor que ahoga,
un dolor que se dulcifica en tu mirada
y por eso es más doloroso.
Quiero decir tu nombre, papá.
Quiero odiarte
para que no duela el dolor con que te llamo.

La memoria tortura,
la memoria aterra.

En lo blanco, lo blanco.
Luz que gotea murmullos silentes.
Y en lo blanco, tu cuerpo dolorido
como *Cristo, uomo dei dolori*
mientras tu sangre mana incontenible.

    Tu sangre negra, tu sangre blanca, tu sangre roja,
    tu sangre hiel y azúcar, tu sangre pedernal y chispa.
    Tu sangre que nos une, que nos mata,
    que se derrama a torrentes
    sobre la negra blancura del hospital.

Luego la noche y sus temores.
El rezo, el grito, la no resignación
porque aún sigues en mí,

porque aún no caes en el olvido,
porque no te quiero muerto.
Es julio, papá.
Hace seis meses y sigue lloviendo.

-Rosa Mendoza-Valencia

Babel

En mi casa aúlla el viento
y ya no florecen los limoneros.
Las tejas resbalan, monótonas,
una sobre otra,
se precipitan y caen
a un abismo de gatos muertos.
La tristeza barre los rincones
y hay un abandono doloroso en las cosas.
Unas cuantas ramas,
plañideras andrajosas,
elevan su llanto mudo al cielo
 y tú no las oyes.

El eco de tus pasos aún retumba en las paredes
y se pierde en la sombra de las palabras no dichas,
de las lágrimas no lloradas
de los adioses sin sentido.
¿Cómo recordarte, Babel?
¿Cómo decir tu nombre sin que duela
 si estás presente en cada latido?

Desde tu partida,
el fuego de mi hogar está apagado.
Desde que no estás,
soy una casa de relojes descompuestos ,
de tiempo detenido,
de luces apagadas.
Una casa en la que ya nunca
florecen los limoneros.

-Rosa Mendoza-Valencia

tortillas en el comal

     poco chamuscadas
y frijolitos en la olla.

la jefita, con su delantal
y el jefito saboreando su cafecito —
los dos, platicando,
     recordando aquellos tiempos.

los perros ladran y rasguñan la tela
"dale de comer a esos perros", ella le dice,
       "ya vas a empezar", él responde.

y entre el arrullo de palomas
       y sonidos de las campanas de la iglesia
   a la distancia
      llamando a los fieles,

"no te vayas que ya mero está el lonche",
   ella implora
y él, ni se despide,
      y menos con un beso

desde adentro,
   se oye el zumbido de la troca.
      ella sale a regar su jardín.
       y a darle su lonche

     y su bendición.

-Paul Pineda

Entonces se les abrieron

los ojos
se vieron
solos
y dieron vida
raíz nueva
en tierra
eterna
fresca y húmeda
compañía
la del amor.

Sentencia eterna:
te dolerás
de tus ramas
sufrirás
las lluvias no vendrán
el sol no será más
bendito
las heridas por sus llamas
costarán
tu verdor.

Los ojos se miraron
desnudos
pronunciaron
el perdón.
Nunca se marchitaron
de dar
vida.

-Héctor Limón

Yo soy

Soy la **tristeza** de dejar todo lo que era mío en México.

Soy el **olor** de sopa de fideo con frijoles de olla recién hechos por mi madre.

Soy el **sabor** de una concha con una taza de chocolate caliente "la abuela".

Soy la **risa** que me sale cuando veo al Chavo del 8 y la Chilindrina.

Soy los **sueños** que mis padres trajeron con ellos acompañados.

Soy la humilde **maleta** llena de esperanza que me acompañó al cruzar la frontera.

Soy el **sudor** de la frente de mis padres.

Soy las **ampollas** que brotan en nuestras manos mientras trabajamos en las labores.

Soy **el español** que sale de mi boca cuando digo "te quiero".

Soy **el español** que me conecta con mi cultura y mi identidad.

Soy **el inglés** que tuve que aprender en la escuela para que me entendieran.

Soy las **humillaciones** que sufrí por ser mejicana.

¡Y por todos esto – hoy **soy doctora**!

-Dra. Matilde A. Sarmiento-Arribalzaga

Choked Chalks Flying in The Air

Teachers threw all their magic marks
Out of the window and went home
Their starved ears had been patient
Only to become the lies' dance-floor
They were the uncarpeted base
In a nightclub of famine and fools
They trooped out, unprepared
And unable to dance to the disco
Of peanuts and pauperization
Fibs were played as an addition
To the dancing of folly and failings
Their restaurant reserved for none
But hunger, helplessness & hardships

-Ndaba Sibanda

Mediocre

There once was a boy of average everything who walked through his childhood with terrible eyesight. As a child he would squint, and strain his eyes to see. His forehead became a mass of wrinkles and his eyes set deeper and deeper beneath them. The world demanded to be seen. With his limited vision, stray dogs in his unremarkable neighborhood transformed into werewolves, butterflies were fairies and birds became dwarfed pterodactyls. Mice scratching behind the walls of his small house were actually the dead trying to communicate with him. People in his life would tell him what things really were. The way they saw the world was very bland. Believing them, the boy grew disillusioned and as things lost their luster the world became less and less worthy of squinting. The wrinkles on his forehead became lax and covered his eyes completely.

-Ignacio Ibarra

Border Crossing 1993

Citizenship? Oh It's you again.

Yes sir.

Where are you going?

I'm on my way to school.

What was your business in Mexico?

I live there/ My grandma was sick/ I was buying cigarettes.

Wait. You live in Mexico and you are going to school in the US?

Yes sir. I told you that yesterday and the day before.

Don't you know it's against the law?

No it's not.

It is. I can hold you here till your parents come get you.

My parents do not have a phone. You are going to make me late. Again.

I don't give a shit if you are late.

Woah. I'm just a kid trying to get to school. You are a grown man.

Doesn't matter.

It should. I've established my citizenship, may I please go to school?

You got drugs on you? What's in that water bottle?

Water.

You think you are real smart, don't you?

No I don't. That's why I'm going to school.

Don't let me see you here again.

I can't help it if you are here every morning making me late.

Get lost.

See you tomorrow.

Get out.

Bye.

-Ignacio Ibarra

Dad's Silhouette

I reached out and touched
my father's silhouette.
I jolted
as if I could go no further.
I awoke in the dark den
laying in the lounge chair.
Turned on the lamp and the
room was silent.

-Danny P. Barbare

SPRING

peeps in like a
voyeur clown with
pale green grunts

of juggled earth
riding bareback
in a dappled field

wearing its tent
of crawling skin
as the sun appears

and shakes the air awake
its voices trying out
some light on their

yet virgin tongues.

-Askold Skalsky

SPINNERS

Enter the room,
the bright walls painted
with happiness.
Come in like a fountain
of light meeting light.
Open the window
to bring the fragrant air,
the blue green drafts
of billowy sunlight
streaming into the white
sheets.

Welcome, Gladicita.

Here at last we shall sit
like happy hermits
in transparent cowls,
our bodies glowing,
naked with sunshine,
spun and spinning
the golden thread
in our hands,
our empty hands,
measureless and brimful
with blossom-bearing
fruit.

-Askold Skalsky

REPOSE IN ADVERSITY

My Calamity, my Jane, my Shakti
of the West, ride down from your bright
theater's screen that I first saw
in the high mesas of South Jersey's
flatland marl, and calm yourself.
Undo your bangles, your horrific holster's
barrel-eye of lead. You've assailed me,
outdrawn me, and out-whipped me,

and what now? We're still ranging over
the tumbleweeds of tumbling light, saddled
with the desert places of our possibilities.
Come. Let us sit and rest a moment in another
country in the midst of this immensity
and touch the open spaces of the heart.

-Askold Skalsky

Forests Born Under Sky Dreams

When the early whispers of autumn
Fly gaily through our home
On the wind's strings
In small, delicate symphonies
We spill our bodies on the bed
Crawl between freshly washed cotton sheets
And twist our limbs into unorganized knots
We nibble on the last of our summer frenzies
Memories of berry picking
In warm July and August
Trying to taste the garden-fresh
Sweet juices of the raspberries
Blueberries, blackberries
That burst on our tongues
Between teeth and roused taste buds

But before we swallow autumn's bounty
Hot spiced ciders, baked goods with cloves
Cinnamon, nutmeg, allspice
Before the fall gifts her delicate presents
Floods of cinnabar, fire opal, honey topaz
To the rolling forests along Skyline Drive
Backbone of Shenandoah National Park
Let us kiss with our words in bed, until
Our tongues are tickled and pulsing
Let the moans escape from our lungs
Vibrating into the shadows
Of the year's last summer nights

-Sarah Joy Thompson

True Like Time

There was a bit of calm before the traffic
But the evening rush hour mirrored us
Frantic, drunk, lusting
For high seas in the summer
Wanting to be enormously wild
Like innocent children clutching
The language of untainted joy
In our mouths, on our tiny tongues
Small hands holding salt water
Shimmering specks of light
When we could inhale, exhale
Time… and youth was a typo
Repeated too frequently
Omitted too easily

Youth became a fragment
Elusive like words we forgot to say
Or didn't repeat often enough
I love you I love you I love you
A run-on sentence
Then a full stop
Time… all lives fragile

Building my first ofrenda
For Dia de Muertos this year
To place my father's picture upon
Put things into perspective
No matter how we try to suppress
The notion of getting older, duller
Moments pour out of our eyeballs

With a few drinks
At family gatherings

And we feel tricked by the minutes
And we cannot stop time

-Sarah Joy Thompson

Waiting for Winter

Sliding door ajar
listening to December winds
pick up speed as the last yellowed leaves
outside our window lose their grip
and scantily clad branches
form proscenium arches
botanical theatres
framing this gray show
beyond the glass

As I step outside
the approaching season
comes with icy breath
touching the neck
biting extremities, my fingers go numb
alternating between one hand
in the pocket of my parka
one hand around the dog leash

My body halted
by the unpredictable cold
I feel so much like an old tree
which has been through landslides
the soil shaken at my roots
almost toppled over
my bark deliberately invaded
by lichens and mosses

But still I choose to grow upright

splash grounding water on my face
something rose-scented with murumuru
to remind me of my siblings in California
resting a hand against
a younger sister's cheek
to produce perfect liquid lines
of eyeliner on soft eyelids
or a troop of us frolicking
through trails that lead
to Redwood fairy rings
or the hollows of giant trees
staying up late in the kitchen
to talk things over
to talk over each other
to laugh, be heard, seen

At least there is reminiscing
to make our winter
not so cold after all

-Sarah Joy Thompson

Notas escritas al margen del cuaderno negro sobre Charcot

3

Pétrea huesa podrida
en la angosta sombra de la noche.
Charcot pisa los charcos
de densa mierda parisina.
Sus delgados pasos dejan rastro
hasta el hospital de la Salpêtrière.

Ahí lo reciben tiernamente
sus dóciles perras histéricas,
seres cuyo útero mutaba
en la gran bestia negra.

Animales sin alma con vaginas dentadas,
devoradoras de inmundicias,
poéticas, ladran, contorsionándose
en el bramante sueño
de la ola galopante de sí mismas.

Arriba en la piel hirviente
del oscuro cielo parisino,
el pez de la noche
brilla triangular.

4

Charcot pensaba en las heces
más blandas del cerebro,
el impulso eléctrico del trauma,
la contorsión del cuerpo
como animal incendiado.

El cuerpo como poema destrozado,
violado y desmembrado
por los poetas de la médica rabia.

El dolor forzado a ser espectáculo,
la imagen consumible de un catálogo
de la enajenación histérica de la carne.

-Esther M. García

Alteración cerval de la conciencia

Su lenguaje es el delirio,
castiga con los súlfures mares de su lengua.
Belleza que rompe por atravesamiento
del lenguaje.

Dice la enfermera
-define el trauma-
y enumera la simetría de la catástrofe:
un padre que acaricia
por las noches a su hija.

Una mano es una mano
pero también los dedos,
la presión, el dolor, la herida.

Dolor amputado,
miembro fantasma que habita
el convulsionado cerebro.

Recuerdo sepultado.
Un muerto apesta el cadáver
de la ahora viva.

Trauma es la seducción,
la mano que lanza el golpe,
el golpe y el impacto
que no dejó cicatriz,
o herida física.

Por dentro, la memoria ejecuta
el rito sombrío;
la rememoración oculta, siniestra.

-Esther M. García

Yūgen

Deep into a gloom and doom of a restless night
it started raining heavily,
the sky was black as a cauldron.
The cuckoo clock rang maliciously two or three times:
and the bark of restless neighbor dogs
was getting lost more and more
in the bitter rumble of menacing flashes in the sky.
Lightning ripped the sky into countless
extremely bright blue-light intertwined nets,
randomly covering every part of the sky;
- under the auspices of night and imagination -
quite like the fluorescent webs of giant spiders up in the sky.
Heavy raindrops running in a strong drumming rhythm
bouncing back and forth against different surfaces.
A composition made of a slight staccato rhythm
is interspersed with the climax of the crescendo
given by the rumble in the sky.
After a while, all the fuss and commotion
were gradually reduced as if someone
had pointed a huge remote controller up towards the sky
and was constantly pressing the volume down button.
At the same time, a huge tapestry
of thick black clouds spreads out in one spot,
looking almost as if someone deliberately
tore it apart in that particular place:
and oh my, look - a thin but resolute
beam of silver moonlight finding its way
through the overwhelming thick darkness
that seeks to practically stifle it.

All of a sudden, I couldn't help
but think about life itself -
that accustomed matrix of ours:
quite similar to this magnificent
and awe-inspiring performance
that took place up in the sky.

-Dušan Pejaković

Border Angels

545 angels,
umbilical cords severed
for a second time
because they held
their parent's hand
across an artificial line
in the shifting sand.
They wander
aimlessly because
bookkeepers
and caretakers
wouldn't write it down,
kept it in their heads
and threw away
the keys. Corralled
and caged
until they can
lose enough weight
to slip through
the bars.

-Stephen Schwei

Pathogen Pause

As we attempt to glide past each other
in a supermarket meeting of the aisles,
we both pause to keep our distance,
a medically-designated six feet or more.
We dare not touch or breathe the same air.
I try to navigate to avoid anything close,
like a robot with vision sensors
seeing the people around me like objects,
pathogen-bearing, potentially lethal
carriers that must be avoided.

I used to gravitate to people, even willing
to hug, hold hands, or soften with a kiss,
but now I evade like the plague-ridden
malicious temptresses they are.
In the grocery store, we both hesitate,
our carts caught in the pathogen pause,
where any movement forward
can only be attempted if there's a safe path.
We used to smile, but now we're tense,
both trying to escape the creeping contagion.

-Stephen Schwei

Lag

When you realize,
'Please return the library books
They're on the table'
As her last words
Balances every "I love you" she'd given

Instead of goodbye
The incessant, familiarity of instruction
 the sum

                                        of my mother

-Allison Whittenberg

Larceny

Charlatan queen
That veil over your face is wearing thin
Your eyes shine through like smooth amethyst crystals
Radiating your identity, ratting you out
You can try your best to cleanse your soul
Before exile is handed down
Sentence endowed by a jury of your peers
Your falsified aptitude has uncloaked itself
True expertise plagiarized by insecurity
Blind attempts to snag luck's blessing have finally missed the target
Literary opuses forged by quills in fixated hands tell master class tales
Narratives that live outside your artistry's realm give your secrets away
Regret falls on blind ears
Wear your scarlet letter proud; karma's honest gift is your true treasure
You should have known better than to play with fire
Your rumination hangs like a grey cloud
Your contrition tattooed across your chest
Maybe next time you'll think twice
Before you play fool's hands in a card shark arena
It's only a game, after all

-Jamie Santomasso

GRAVITY UNGRATEFUL

Yes, I am dressed in mourning
Dark clothes for a dark time
Yet I yearn to escape
Pandemic imprisonment
With the germ of an idea
That will allow me to soar
Above my confinement
In an airborne threat
Against complacency and boredom
As I reach up to a blue heaven
That promises social distancing
On a cosmic scale,
But that old bitch gravity
Bears down on me,
Slapping me down
Like a petulant child
Crying out
For what she cannot have,
Slammed back
To a blanketed earth
Of red, white, and blue.

-Mark Blickley

Daily Life

We anchor the high hill
in daily life
occasionally look down at
people passing by
moving
the dust of daily life

They sigh
the net of daily life is too dense
there is no vacant land
to accumulate dust
cannot but swallow
a handful of dust everyday
cleaning up a vacant land
in their own chests

Occasionally look down at
the crowd of people
they have learned how to move
their own dust as well

Sigh in the same manner
for not enough vacant land
swallow in the same manner
dust constantly generated

Day after day
everyone swallows each other's dust
and accumulates each other's dust
in one's own chest

-Yu-Hsuan Wu

Don't Speak My Name When I Am Gone

Don't speak my name when I am gone
Your tears would scar the earth
Eliminate the starred sky
Eviscerate the dirt
Don't speak my name when I am gone
Your cry would dry the sea
Split atoms into empty heat
Through salty gravity
Forget my name when I am gone
The sounds that held me whole
Vibrating streams of syllables
By bell's bellowing toll
Forget my name when I am gone
Forget you ever heard
The music that composed my life
Embodied in that word
So dry your eyes to save the skies
Preserve the whirling world
Don't speak my name when I am gone
To let Creation still unfurl

-Stephen Douglas Wright

¿De dónde eres?

you ask us
>   where we're from

how do i explain it to you
>   in a way you might understand

you see, where we come from is
>   as much a place
>   as it is a time.

a place you never had to be
>   nor a time you ever had to know

we are from that holy place
>   where nuestros antepasados salieron,
>   formados por las tierras que pisaron
para llegar aquí.

We are from that wicked, wicked place
>   donde aprendimos
>   a tragarnos la rabia
y sufrir los desaires y dolores
>   del racismo .

you ask us where we are from
>   we are from the side of town
with roads you didn't have to walk -
>   the ones without a sidewalk;
we are from the pothole-filled streets

and neighborhoods without utilities -
the ones
you never knew existed.

So, when we answer your question,
          no te aguites, ese.
we got over it
          a long time ago.

we just don't ever want to forget
               de donde somos .

-Paul Pineda

She Gobbled the Fast Foods

I was worried. She eats only fast food. Fries, hamburgers, kebabs.

Unfortunately, the effects of the diet were already visible - the fold was chasing the fold. Soon she will turn into a Michelin man...

I decided to act.

- Imagine that you are eating something new. Exotic taste. Delicate, melting in the mouth, but with a hint of something, which you do not recognize. - I talked inspired. - There are so many possibilities. Aren't you tempted to try something new?

- I am.

The next day she bought frozen fries.

- Honey! - She was smiling. - You convinced me. I bought another brand of ketchup!

-Krzysztof Dąbrowski

Stitching the World

Hopes and dreams crumbled
       others ravaged by floods
              alone they wait hopelessly—

this world does not forget...
       human cruelty
              racial discrimination
gentrification
       nationalization
              dehumanization.

Poverty, the hollowness
       consumes our hearts.
              We wish the ills of the world

will slither away,
       shoved into a dark place.
              Where darkness becomes light

where bugs, leaves and lilies
       tell poetic stories
              to the wind.

And the hum of hummingbirds
       distracts the butterflies
              and bees from buzzing.

Every song is just a thimble
    like the needle moving
        on the cloth pattern of life

creating   the   next   stitch.

-Raúl Sánchez

Heritage

Loud voices resound from east to west
all lives matter was the call,
echoed among the people manifesting,
protesting perpetual injustices.

Exploitation, extraction, thievery from people
who knew not what their ancient soil harbored.
Simple people, laborious, engaged, noble.
Foreign power invaded the territories they preserved.

Ancient travelers guided by the stars
sailing unknown oceans. Fearless they roamed
to find flat land. Myth dissolved on earth's scars.
Spanish, British, Portuguese alike pleased their kings.

Conquered, subjugated, raped, killed the natives.
Uneducated, unqualified, unwanted people they thought,
"We will teach you, guide you. Our cross at hand will
bless you, our religion will save you, have faith, they said."

Criollos, Mulatos, Mestizos, Castizos,
Zambos, Pardos, Albinos,
Araucanos, Moriscas, Mapuches, Indios
Cambuja, Loba, Zambaiga, Barcinos

Everyone carries a small percent of that mixed blood.
Their loud resounding voices remind us,
we're part of this world, our world.
Our blood united, our fighting voices

united, demanding justice for all, right now!

-Raúl Sánchez

If My Hands Could Talk

Born naked, without religion
my hands shook in cold air
away from my mother's womb

my small arms and hands
wrapped up bundled up—
to suck my mother's nipples

to nourish my existence.
Those hands, my hands
have created, nourished, built,

repaired, edified, embraced,
shook other people's colored hands.
My hands do not have gunpowder

or somebody else's blood.
My folded hands have worshipped,
demigods and deities in faraway countries.

My hands raise in protest
against racial injustice
my hands wave the liberty banner

my hands write poems
for the world to read.

-Raúl Sánchez

We Fight to Win

We work with fingers in the earth for mind breaths.
We work online prompts and vespetro meetings.
Dogs and cats, our vespers through COVID-19 nights.
We are fighting for our lives —

Subtle loneliness creeps in — like a sweetly perfumed
beast laden with a blood-stained club fresh off the tanning bed
thumping our senses before pummeling our bodies
          — but we fight, we fight to win.

All our bad days, our catastrophes, our Black Sundays,
our days of infamy, our assassinations, our dropped towers,
our overrun sacred lands, our dragged into the streets
dead — leave us utterly forlorn.

But — this 'good earth' still rotates
          — spinning through space around a star.
We'll get off the floor, the couch and out into
that bright light to raise our voices to fight on.

For whom do we fight? For the economy? *NO!* What is money
but a means of corrupt power. For the kids and grandkids.
The elderly who've been told to sacrifice their lives.
We fight for love and dignity; we will win.

-Tom Murphy

Poem 2

Breakfast over, e mails done so a family walk in the sun
Watch the little man run, I'm thinkin'
How nice to get away out of the house for part of the day
Then it's back to compose some more, another score
Lookin' on facebook an' I see to my delight a 6 month old baby won her coronavirus fight
Allaying fears, article said nurses in tears an' I know it meant
Tears of Joy at their achievement,
Cos' it was thought she would not survive much longer
But she was kept alive eventually proving the stronger
And I knew in the end when we win through so many would owe
So much to the underpaid, understaffed, undervalued, overworked few
An' put it on facebook for all to see, an' some who did agreed with me
Then a video of a deer frolicking, enjoying itself in the surf on an isolated seashore
Like a child seeing the sea for the first time and so wrote the following rhyme
"Running free by the sea, a deer frolicked on the sea shore
Later the humans returned and it was seen no more"
Which made me feel blue cos' it would probably be true
Then a request at someone's behest
Can I record and send a poem I wrote, it was a score
About workin' with a guy who's with us no more
It was done an' sent off it went hopefully later I'll be able to watch it and see

Myself in action but for now, it's time for tea

--Trev Wainwright

Written as a day in lockdown unfolded, a day when I would have been in The Valley but for covid, there were no food parcels to be delivered that day. The little man is my nickname for our Boston Terrier Milo, the guy who is with us no more is the late San Antonio Poet Harold Rodinsky, well respected by all who knew him at the RGVIPF

Autumn Equinox
(for David Pesqueira)

Wooden hatchet's handle
smooth from use,
its steady blade
bites an edge off
hard dried log,
reveals striated furrows
in finger-length pieces,
becomes tinder when
tossed on embers.
Insurgent orange-red
whole-flame swallowed,
we greet season's first sun-
rise on this windy shore,
with prayers, sage and
bush-craft skills within
rituals remembered.

-Carlos Cumpián

Calm Panic
(for JXC)

You offer us sonic bread, composed of well-
kneaded beats turn spirals out of triangles,
your electric audio dominance soars, calls up
boisterous ghosts and reshapes them.

Muscle memories bring fingertip calluses
where talent rules-- releases
a roaring Niagara Falls where we drown
in your opus sound playground.

Eyes on you as you levitate the room, take us for
a wild ride down Bryn Mawr reveals a youthful grace
across your face, and smiles on those still combing, going
bald and Q-tip heads which bob to your rhythmic rolling.

All–drunk on note symmetry-winged dreams that zoom across the ceiling,
no one can see the door anymore – prisoners to your cinematic hail storm
volcanic eruption   – snow storm—wind shear—tornado blowing decibels of delight
in the fresh breeze bliss that beckons amid fading summer light.

Asymmetrical danger leaps out at us deep like some shadowy favela,
– on the outside windshields crack at the high notes— piercing drum percussion
without warning, we soar above eagles and satellites, you give keyboard permission for lift off in savage illumination.

-Carlos Cumpián

Most Won't Have Krishnamurti's Crown

Once you hit 50 and if your hair
brush still has its original purpose
you're one lucky S.O.B.
you might say you won the genetic lottery, so stop
watching wig commercials, it's crazy to believe
in onion juice cures rubbed on the scalp
will make you delicious with curls, plus you'll smell.
Maybe there's no laser savior, special red space light
technology to grow hair back in the twenty-first century;
all you'll need are deep pockets, a heaven for credit card
wishe$ so go on line, or phone to seek victory over
the receding Neanderthal nest that some Sasquatch
big foot might show you how to maintain that modern
comb dome covered with protein shafts,
as the civilized bastards hoist their stadium of baseball
caps while howling with indignation.

-Carlos Cumpián

The M Word

For Gil Scott-Heron

Don't act like this is the first time I betray you on the page. Remember the pregnant mother on the border poem that met with feverish applause? Remember how it was followed by the hungry peyote bisexual poem that met with murderous silence? Me too.

I know you have a reasonable expectation of dulcet danzas and daring diatribes hurled like sand in the face of Whitey with his crackity cracks and truckity sacks, where señoras and their weathered brown hands are to gambol in milpas with corn husks, perchance to smug. Listen, I don't want this either. Trust.

But this isn't the blood and maguey sector of Aztlán, at the intersection of raised fist and groomed goatee. This is the weeping district, on the corner of lo cagué y lo cagamos.

Funny. How we didn't speak Spanish but still had certain words stuck in our mouths, durable signifiers, crooked, but they got it done in a pinch. Cachetón. Big cheeked. Puro pedo. I swear to god if it wouldn't make me a raging antisocial and scare my students I would tattoo it on my knuckles: pure fart. Chale. Pachuco for no way josé. Gacho. All the way fucked up wrong. Gabacho. Our word for Whitey, as in: The man jus' upped my rent las' night / cause gabacho's on the moon / No hot water, no toilets, no lights. / but gabacho's on the moon.

Órale. Órale should have been the first one in the primer ¿no? I've heard órale vato translate to come on dude or right on man but these sound terrible. At the root, orar is to pray. Pray for it as in: testify, preach.

Then there's the M bomb.
I just thought mayate meant Black. I thought it sounded cool, like Panama hats or jazz.
So I used it.
It does not mean Black.

It made Beto laugh. The best popper in our grade, I liked him even though I was bookish and he was bad. Not quite a cholo, but certainly cholo adjacent.

I didn't say it again, backing out of the pleasure it offered, even though a book girl holds nothing more precious than the shekel in her purse she can trade for a bad boy's grin.

Later I discovered it's the Mexican word for dung beetle. The barrio N word has an exoskeleton and eats excrement. A word like huffing glue so you don't feel your fingers when they send you to pull the trigger on a stranger.

Errant bombs of sad cachetones.
Pray for it.

-Paloma Martínez-Cruz

Merchola

For Lizzo

Merchola with diaphanous skin
marooned in tires and glass
she sings to me:
she loves her love with a letter p
for plastic bags and license plates
for packing peanuts and pesticides

Her voice an earfeel of tadpole and rebar
her kisses goldfish pucker exes and ohs
ensnared in deep sea nets
set to simmer, cooking

Jump me in won't you
for me la vida ichthyoloca
we'll pillar of salt their necks till they snap
our fish cloacas set to stun
they could have had a sea bitch, effulgent
they could have had a planet
they have a dingy

-Paloma Martínez-Cruz

POEM FOR MITKO

Today, when Ziggy
(the dog) and I
go down to the ocean
we'll send you a poem

Some wild ribbon
invisible soul
birds in flight
across chrome waters

We will wait
for your silent reply
Look for a word
And world of peace

Riding back
over bright breakers
From your land-
locked European country

*

A Sea-Monkey
I was born and raised
in Florida

Learned my liquid life
Now, I am pulled

by the moon

Birth and inevitability
Yes, the ocean
Gives us power

Tells us the rolling universe
Does not belong to us
No matter how hard

We try to destroy it

*

Godless power
Chrome waves

Sun's flames
soak my brow

Ziggy stops to dig in the sand
Barks at the blue-black raven

Calling from the stranded
Boulder on Shell Beach

*

I'd go crazy living on an island

Surrounded by a fevered sea of woe

And sapphire horizons

I plan for a busier tomorrow
But I can't get the ocean out of my head

You could crave another island

But whatever's there I can't describe
Lupine, thistle, and wild oats

On the bluff
Something I think I see, but can't

Imagination
Inscribed in the mercurial sky

I wait for an explosion

*

This is not a good year for Tyrants!
Copper skies above Tahrir Square

Here comes that crashing thought
That currency I sent away over the expanse

To be read by you, Mitko
Tear gas clouds in Tahrir Square

Coming back tied and frayed around a rugged headland
We have had enough of this enslavement!

Men and women, boys and girls with stones
Give them what they want

Don't wait for permission from the headquarters
Authorization from the Opera

Live long and without endorsements

*

The dog still barks, but can't say exactly what he believes
Is that a dragon or civilization burning on the beach?

Coming in or going out
I can't tell which way the poetry is running

A wave followed by another wave followed by another
A sleeper wave

Tide of the underworld rushing overall, blowing silver
Over shipwrecked shores and tortured skies

*

I asked the California badger
on the road back home
Do you find this dream amusing?

There was something vicious in his response
Is the human condition just entertainment?

I ask the badger
about political gamesmanship
and coppery metaphors

Slung across the heavens
like Handel's Messiah?

No reply!

This is not a domestic animal!

*

O, Brother from another great continent
Beyond shimmering cataclysmic fever

Foam and light rushing up over my feet
Mammoth rubbings on mammoth stones. . .

Oh Macedonian Brother

I went down to the ocean today and the sky and sun and water
were blinding and gorgeous chrome, so I kind of got caught

in light and isolation and could think of nothing else.

                                    12.28.2011

-Michael Rothenberg

END OF JANUARY

1

Rain, creak, rush, break
Leak in the roof

Another baptism
Crowns a Jew

Gash and smoke

Bare legs brace and bend
Against a wobbling street

Poetry and silk. . .

2

17,000 slot machines

One quarter: no inspiration
Two dollars: a drop of grace
Ten dollars: a tease, tug, love/hate
Twenty dollars: chance fails

Try the buffet

3

Drive & Park
Park & Sleep
Sleep & Fly
Fly & Fly
& Fly

Go nowhere. Get there
The end

4

Rain and palm trees soak my sleep
Few stars, no moon

Dream
Beyond The breakers
My father navigates an open boat
Without running lights
Through rough seas to find a restaurant
And runs aground in the shallows

5

Windows fall out of a crumbling head

A naked man on a bicycle points at a broken eye
Skewered by the wind

Puppies scream from a car
Pre-dawn insomnia whiplash

Astroturf gardens populate
Both ends of the world

Until the director says, "Cut"
And sends the cast out for empanadas

6

"Coo-koo"
"Coo-koo"

Translucent blue bottles
A couple dozen Hollywood crows

7

Vegetation sucks at my feet
José Martí, García Lorca, clouds
In the cabbage palm.

-Michael Rothenberg

THE RAINY SEASON

for Michael McClure

By morning, as love
moves through the rain,

a gray squirrel forages sodden ground,
disrupts lacy ferns, heavy oak leaves
and pine needle mulch

Salamanders rest
in gold pools below deadwood
in the mossy creek bed.

Soggy winter
has its resurrecting reign
over the weak and great,
delicious and repugnant sporophytes.

Blue jays gorge at the feeder.
Varied thrush whistle in a minor key
among dense thickets.

And the rain, rain bounces
on clouds, roof deck, cracked
asphalt drive, seeps from serpentine
outcroppings and perilous
slides all along the dark
and never-ending river road.

At night giant redwoods inhale
They know the rain will come

January 4, 2015

-Michael Rothenberg

Adentro

Siento, presiento
y me pongo a cuentas conmigo mismo
que a diario me sumo lo que vivir descuenta,
respiros…

Dos sentires humanos
probablemente estuve en la luz
antes de que me dieran a luz,
se amaron…

De rastros y rostros
ideas, pensares y sueños
lleno estoy de lo que llena a la vida,
momentos…

Adentro, un influjo infinito
despiértame el cuerpo a la luz cada día
a diario me infunde una cuota de vida,
y existo…

-Eduardo Rosero

De ti

Te digo amor
cuando no lo digo
y dejo caer un beso en tu frente,
cuando en total silencio
tomo tu mano,
y el alma mía te lleva del alma…

Digo te amo
cuando sin palabras
te habla mi voz y tus ojos entienden,
cuando contigo
solo un abrazo
y sostengo todo mi universo…

Digo te quiero
cuando menos lo digo
y estoy para ti,
cuando más me precisas,
cuando no eres más que solamente miedo
y te cuido conmigo y te abrazó la vida…

Te digo amor
aunque no lo diga
y vuelvo a elegirte todas las veces
porque solo contigo
los dos de la mano
y el alma de ti me tiene del alma…

-Eduardo Rosero

No sé si te invento

Tú caminas por calles
que yo no conozco.
Pisas duro o despacio en tu vieja ciudad.
Ni siquiera te veo o lo sé.
Yo no sé cómo ríes ni lloras
(aunque he oído tu llanto).
Solo tengo el recuerdo de un tiempo
tu risa de infancia
que ya se nos fue.
No conozco tus malas palabras
las noches de insomnio
tus ganas de amar o morir
las puertas que tocas
el niño que salvas.
Vivo a expensas de un largo "no sé".
Yo no sé si me quieres al menos
ni si al cabo de un rato
ayer o mañana
te aburrirás de mí.
Yo no veo tu cielo con nubes.
No adivino ni el grito que ocultas.
Yo no siento tu frío en la piel.
No percibo el olor de tu aire
las voces que escuchas
sus timbres y acentos.
Yo no sé si me mientes…
Si mientes.
Yo no sé si te invento…
O si existes.
Y hoy no sé si te quiero.

-Barbarella D´Acevedo

I do not know if I'm making you up

You walk streets
That are unknown to me.
You stomp hard or tread lightly in your old town.
I don't even see you and I don't know.
I don't know how you laugh or cry
(Although I have heard your cry).
I only have the memory of a time
Of your childhood laughter
That has already gone.
I don't recognize your bad words
The sleepless nights
Your desire to love or to die
The doors that you knock on
The child that you save.
I live at the expense of a long "I don't know."
I don't know if you at least love me
If after a while
Yesterday or tomorrow
You will get bored of me.
I don't see your cloudy skies.
I don't suspect the cries that you hide.
I don't feel your coldness on my skin.
I don't smell the essence of your air
The voices that you hear
Their sounds and accents.
I don't know if you lie to me
If you lie.
I don't know if I'm making you up…
Or if you exist.
And today I don't know if I love you

-Barbarella D´Acevedo

Esas cosas pequeñas

A veces una solo
requiere
de lo simple.
A veces.
Una canción absurda.
Leer un chiste sucio.
Tardar en sonreír.
Precisa una
tan poco.
Sin notas trascendentes.
Ni una lluvia de astros…
Si acaso
un, ¿cómo estás?
¿Y el clima?
¿Llueve mucho?
Conversar de deporte,
los dolores, el fútbol,
las vacunas.
Mis flores.
O tu almuerzo.
Ya sabes.
Esas cosas pequeñas.
Tan sencillas.
Sin dramas.
Lo común.
A veces una busca
no al amante…
Al amigo.

-Barbarella D´Acevedo

Accidente

Una patada en la barriga
un accidente
un colgar de cabeza
en el abismo
sangre
un perderse en lo oscuro
de la vía de un tren
naufragar de mi lancha
y ya sin isla
piel
descarrilarme claro
el picarme una avispa
en el espejo
huesos
un aborto
sin hijo
quedarme destrozada
con el cuerpo de oro
y no morir
descarnada
con fiebre
y hecha miel
descascarada
absurda
todo eso me ocurrió
cuando te amé.

-Barbarella D´Acevedo

Interpretation, not translation, is what becomes poetry.

New Day Dawn

The windchimes quelled with leaden silence.
The stars shone glory in their predawn dusk.
My footsteps rustled, crunched the tumbled leaves
briskly crackling beneath the overhanging eaves.
The wolf dog sniffed the stillborn air,
searching for his morning prey.
Of course he knew he had no chance of darting past,
pouncing on that rabbit ambling o'er the trellis fast,
or the squirrel scampering up the tree limb.
The quiet of the morning air lay thick as fog descending
yet soon the sun would break its silent inkwell,
would streak its loveliness in streams of joy and warmth,
reminding me that even when days' toil is heavy plight,
these morning walks are miracles that flaunt a new day's flight.

El amanecer

Las campanillas de viento sofocan el silencio brusco.

Las estrellas brillan su gloria en el crepúsculo antes del amanecer.

Mis pasos retumban, crujen las hojuelas caídas,

desmoronándolas bajo los aleros colgantes.

El perro lobo olfatea el aire muerto,

buscando su presa matutina.

Por supuesto sabía que no tenía chance de fugarse,

abalanzándose sobre el conejo que ronda por el enrejado,

o la ardilla que corretea por la rama del árbol.

El silencio que sopla en la mañana se espesa como la aminorada niebla

Lucirá su belleza en corrientes de gozo y calidez,

recordándome que cuando los labores son difíciles,

Estos paseos de madrugada son milagros alardeando la primera luz.

-Ana Fores-Tamayo

Memory

"That's the tricky thing about dementia
I know the memory is there
I can feel it
But when I go to access it
It's blocked"
He wears a leather jacket
and slippers with socks
He still tries all things
to make his wife laugh
She's having none of it

-Soren Ramsey

We the Broken

We are whole, we
are broken, we
mend ourselves back together.

We get cheated on, lied to
we become
simple back-up plans
like old crumpled, dusty receipts found
in the bottom of some drawer.

We cry, we
laugh, we scream,
we hate, we love,
we age. We become

somebody's door mat. We raise
our voices to make the noise
stop, yet we try to be not as loud, we
try not to be a bother.

We come back to where
they've hurt us
the most, we
stay to keep the peace.

We tuck our troubles, our doubts, our insecurities away, for
them to never see the light again.

We let ourselves shatter
into a million little pieces while
being able to put ourselves back
together without them noticing
the tiny cracks left.

We let all these things happen
and still we thrive.

-Marisol Adame

Obsesiva tecnología

Y los ojos se restriegan
con la pantalla
mientras el tiempo huye...

Y los dedos coquetean
con el teclado
mientras los momentos pasan...

Y la boca lee adormecida
por una pantalla
los textos ignorantes
de la mediocridad
mientras las situaciones desaparecen.

Y el hijo ya no habla con su madre
porque los dedos
y los ojos
yacen secuestrados por
una pantalla
de buen parecer,
pero cuando se extinga su madre
ya no podrá mover
los ladrillos tiernos del pasado...

Y el tiempo pasa
sobre la imagen viva
de la obsesión,

y ahora es un monstruo
con el cuello doblado,
los ojos que no ven,
los dátiles deformados,
la mente entumecida
y una vida rota...

-Eduar Yosniel Pájaro Peña

Scientists estimate that about one million species of animals live in the ocean.
—National Geographic, online

barefoot   on the beach

weaving   through tourist's
cluster & cluck   tight tribal
bands clinging—to stuff
bags full   full
of buckets and shovels
sunscreen and trunks
books shades and smartphones
snacks maps and cash
—turquoise   an umbrella
claims a circumference of sand

turning my back   i stand at this pacific edge
—wave after wave of emerald swell:
   continuous   massive existence

passing by   a young woman
asks her mother:
will we get our money back
if we don't see a whale

i guarantee   if we don't see
beyond this beach
beyond the whale watcher's binoculars
beyond the suntan and the surf
if we don't look deep   there will be

nothing   to keep
nothing   to guarantee

-d. ellis phelps

Eight million metric tons of plastic are dumped into the oceans each year...the equivalent of nearly 57,000 blue whales. By 2050, ocean plastic will outweigh all the ocean's fish.
—conservation.org

maybe i can

a balcony of ears listens but does not hear
silently   the sea becomes a rank bloom
& destiny unwinds   wanting gravity
what did you say   did i say it too

i trusted you   yet under every word—dark nonsense
—cowardice retching like the guilty
what kind of rulers are we
should we throw virgins into the fire

earth yearns   eons crack open
 i tell you   i tell you   now
(as if i could   maybe i can)
with the sea as my witness:

every sip and zip
every single-use toss
every cling-wrapped glass
every sea-turtle trapped

every brain undone
every giant garbage patch
every deadly red tide
every entangled whale

i tell you   i tell you now
i take it all   i take it all
back

-d. ellis phelps

Behold, consider, we are all thy people…holy cities…a wilderness…Zion…
a wilderness, Jerusalem a desolation. —Isaiah 64:9-10

mouth of madness

today rain   scrub jay bathes
—the redbud   her boudoir

gyration of delight   & dust
overruling yesterday's anvil of heat

grace: this earth turns
           leans
             yearns for change

her huge   face —a painted grey shadow
has closed her eyes   to this:

ancient   reign of fire   of blood
mouth of madness   overflowing

stop

we all   drink from this fountain
circling earth: holy holy holy

water

how
can this
be so

-d. ellis phelps

a message from
People for the Ethical Planting of Animals

plant your
cows for
better beef

La calavera de Gregorio Cortez

Gregorio Cortez huía
de cómo trescientos rinches;
y en su interior decía:
«Me persiguen los muy pinches».

Con rifles le meten bala
porque a un cherife dio muerte,
pero es como hierva mala
y lo acompaña la suerte.

Un amigo lo traiciona
y lo mete al calabozo,
pero al juez tanto impresiona
que no mata al revoltoso.

Por él lloran las bonitas,
que logran que lo perdonen.
Les dice: «Gracias, mijitas,
mas me voy. No se ilusionen».

Pero lo sigue la Parca
hasta allá en Nuevo Laredo,
y con veneno lo marca;
y así se murió… sin miedo.

***

-Gabriel González Núñez

Gregorio Cortez's Calavera

When Gregorio Cortez took flight
from three hundred Texas Rangers,
he mumbled, his lips oozing spite:
"Damn them, these pursuing strangers!"

They shoot at him with their rifles
because a sheriff he has killed,
but to him the shots are trifles
and their vengeance goes unfulfilled.

He's sadly betrayed by a friend
just when he's running out of breath,
but the judge does mercy extend
and spares him being put to death.

Pretty women wail over him
until they manage a pardon.
He tells them, "I know this is grim,
but I am leaving. We are done."

But the Reaper is coming up
straight into Gregorio's new home
where one night she poisons his cup;
he died fearless… but all alone.

-Gabriel González Núñez

hombre de raza cósmica

Revolución de nubes   de sueños   You
are here   reach to touch my cheek   so softly
rebirth otro mundo   otra vez
against all limitations, conformities, zeitgeist
Tus ojos de un color no patentado
    share vibrant vida, hot and strong as sunlight   still
Cariño in the curve of your back   que tanto carga
                                    para tus queridos   still

I gulp down your dreams
and feel them in the chubasco rapids of my veins
Wild sorrel mustangs dance their sinew
across your chest, inside your arms
inside each breath   that sings of sunrise, tierra, libertad
Mexican centuries dance like liquid mercury
surfacing across your skin   un desfile   de raza cósmica

Sin verguenza laughter   delicious   rippling   abundant
  like endless cielos celebrando en un baile de gitanos
Wild windblown curls on your head,
  mulatto pirates at high sea   in unknown territories
Nose   straight as a saber
  from some Finn or Nordic castaway on the Spanish coast
Color mestizo de tus cachetes,
  dorado like the sun, like the passions of blood
Y tu corazón   sin límites,
  no bounds, no reservations, puro indio

Hombre de palabra
clothed in eloquence,   in thoughts and
words so delicate I kiss the full flesh of their lips
suck on their tongue   draw you
inside my drumming vientre
into the very pulse
of genesis

-Carmen Tafolla, Ph.D.

Peregrinaciones I

"Ser todo es ser una parte,
el verdadero viaje es el retorno".
- Ursula K. Le Guin, *Los desposeídos.*

En cualquier selva
hay una palabra oculta
en la piel del leopardo.

Me escondo entre las ramas,
repito su ritual
y anclo a mi centro
su instinto de caza;
ahora es presa de mis brazos.

Lo que pronuncian sus latidos
es tan dulce que me acuna.
Regreso a la infancia
donde dios tiene rostro de felino
y sus ronroneos caen con la lluvia.

Los ronroneos se hacen río;
las historias de la corriente
acarician mis párpados
en los que nadie baila.

Una libélula líquida asciende;
el cielo irrumpe en ella
como si quisiera poseerla
por amor al ritmo.

La libélula cae,
y el canto de los pájaros teje una red
para mantenerla a salvo.

-Daniela Pérez Taborda

El corazón es un enjambre de abejas

que huye del humo
buscando un punto de luz,
pero aparecen sombras
y las palabras se marchan
ante el miedo de no hallar
miel en lo profundo.

La oscuridad se ciñe
al rumor del vuelo,
ata su verdad a los latidos:
no siempre será miel,
también, líquidos ocres
curtirán las formas
mientras otras brotarán de astros distantes.

-Daniela Pérez Taborda

Peregrinaciones II

El canto del fuego
transforma la quietud;
una alquimista ha venido
a moldear las dunas de la arena,
a hacerse tambor
para que las tribus hablen
con las presencias del aire.

Tambor de sol,
invoca a mujeres con ojos de gato.

Tambor de sol,
invoca a mujeres con el desierto
en los ojos.

Tambor de sol,
desdibuja geografías.

Tambor de sol,
crea rutas para vuelos nómadas.

Alquimista, tambor de sol,
transforma el fuego en música.

-Daniela Pérez Taborda

Imagining Wilderness

We sit most days on a bench alongside
the trail through scrub juniper and ash,
a few post oaks, in the small patch beyond
more decorative plantings and manicured
lawns of cottages leased to fortunate
residents of this senior living center.

A Red Shouldered Hawk we'd not seen lifted
herself easily to a high branch
above us and searched the brush for lunch
imagining, as we were, a widespread
wilderness remembered from years far gone
and far removed from our well trimmed campus.

-Milton Jordan

An Evening's Vision

On the shard covered beach near Neah Bay
with sunset at your back you stare beyond
three of us waiting at the stone table
across a continent, past wasted, grave
filled land and a generation's buried
hope for lives of cooperation sharing
resources and respect lost in our age.

This sheltered wilderness we enjoy
shrinks as others you remember and
imagine, we're sure, with such long vision.
Your regrets only for your own failures
call up our own and fill our Pacific
vision with long suffering land scattered
beyond our backs as we eat.

-Milton Jordan

Directions to Pozole on Marfil

McDavitt to Arthur, Arthur to 14th street
where *El Buen Gusto Panadería* greets
Southmost road on
a sideways kiss,
a small stretch over International Boulevard,
long drive past
the Dallas Cowboys house
painted blue with a star,
cheering point of *pitadas* on game days
H-E-B's bike overpass where friends buy *postostis*,
then hang a left at McDonald's,
a few blocks down where the road curves
and four immediate rights brings you to 1784 Marfil Drive,
where a warm home and *pozole rojo* wait inside an *olla*
plastic white tables and metal folding chairs outside
in the one-car driveway
limón, cebolla, radishes, and tostadas decorate
the tabletops in white Styrofoam bowls
an ice-chest with *Joya*
you like manzana
the 900-square foot home clean like a *palacio,*
your people greet you with a *beso* and serve you

-G.G. (Giana Gallardo) Hesterberg

Rosario

My mother is a book on the beach,
a smile like sunshine
barefaced, lovely, and brown.
My mother is a Sunday afternoon barbecue,
the smell of mesquite clouds circling our home,
ebony bean pods underfoot.
My mother is The Beatles and rock 'n roll,
dancing in front of the television
to the tunes on MTV.
My mother is a master emcee,
the audience in stitches,
and I, in awe.
My mother is a Bohemian vagabond in a steady stream,
the curves
in my carefully drawn lines.
My mother is a Mesquite tree,
with the deepest roots
planted in Brownsville.
The words of a spoken prayer,
my mother is, *Rosario*.

-G.G. (Giana Gallardo) Hesterberg

Make A Wish

Dark circles, weary bones, and incoherent thoughts.
The doctor exhausted from caring for the sick,
When you give too much, you leave yourself exposed.

A routinely "sick" Mother with her two excessively, compulsively, overconcerned sons,
Sniffing out their prey with the tenacity of a bloodhound,
The scoundrels' not-so-innocuous small talk infiltrates his psyche.

His horn rim spectacles caked over with the mud of his unfulfilled dreams.
Promises of a higher power and wish fulfillment cast him under their spell.
The doctor all too willing to see exactly what they wanted him to see.

The appearance of an apparition,
A tarnished gold-plated lamp from the antique store trash heap,
A dime-store Halloween costume, blue-face, caravan pants, curly wooden clogs.

A highly educated doctor, the bullseye.
An unbelievable, unthinkable, unfathomable scheme.
He fell for it.

The gentle circular massaging of the lamp over and over,

Left residue on his hands and an empty wallet.
These apparitions don't take credit cards.

The genie was out of the bottle.
The forlorn victim having paid a dear price,
Both in cold hard cash and in his own embarrassment.

But worse, he is no closer to having his dreams fulfilled.

-John Johnson

Ways of Looking at Your Hands When COVID is the Conductor

Where is the woman in the long silk gown?
The one with rose-colored rouge on her face,
and a morning-colored diamond
winking from her right ear.
The one who chases music through millennia.

There's a concert in the small hall of my hands.
I perform on the two brown stages,
the dissonant music of splash and swish
as I robustly rub Dial antibacterial soap
into my skin.
The incessant washing and use of hand sanitizer
bleach my palms like O'Keefe's cow skulls,
exposes every line life has etched into my hands.
Once, I thought they were some instrument
of clutching and releasing. Hands cannot be deceived.
They know the ritual of becoming.

Today I write the grackles' story—
the way they congregate before dawn
or after sunset on tree branches, wires or roofs,
fill the air with their song and caw.
Citizens scream for their silence and dissonance.
but do not celebrate resilience in their iridescent feathers.

They are blackbirds, too, just like me.
Am I afraid of my own story—
of the ones who despise my blackness?

Is resilience a weapon? A helmet? A fist?

I stare in the cup of my hands, see no shadows.
This hidden darkness is everything I want to crush.
I want to hold fast to all colorful things
that make me a black woman.

-Loretta Diane Walker

Ask

"Ask children or birds what blackberries taste like."
—Johann Wolfgang von Goethe

Ask children or birds what blackberries taste like.
Ask the frog why it never complains
about the temperature of the pond.
Ask the deer why it risks its life to return home.
Ask the eagle if it's lonely to be majestic.
Ask the bald mulberry if it misses the fallen leaves.
Ask the blowing leaves if they grieve aged limbs.
Ask the spoon the flavor of my tongue.
Ask my bones if they desire strength or beauty.
Ask my blood if it wants to drip or flow.
Ask my lungs what is the meaning of air.

-Loretta Diane Walker

Blame

For my part I know nothing with any certainty, but
the sight of the stars makes me dream."— Vincent van Gogh

Tonight, it is exceptionally quiet
in this loud month of March.
The wind suckles stillness like a pacifier.
I stand on my front porch, beyond my bedtime,
in the pale darkness wondering
do stars dream their light?
Do they try to outperform each other
in the theater of a darkened sky?
Do they blame the Creator
for crafting them night creatures?

What is the stars' language?
Do they speak the same dialect of the eyes
searching the firmaments before they sleep?
Before their tongues are permanently silenced?
Stars have faces too.
Like the natives, the immigrants, the blacks,
the Latinos, the Jews, the disabled, the Buddhists,
the Christians, the Muslims, the agnostics, the atheists,
the Hindus, the homeless, the poor, the mentally
unbalanced… ammunition in the weapon of blame.

Those who aim have faces too.
The farmer, miner, mechanic, bookkeeper, sales clerk,
cotton machine operator, politician, waitress, welder...
making blame a god.

Broken dreams are kindling and hate is gasoline.
The flame of a golden tongue ignites both
for the sake of power. In the fire, death
becomes a way of life masses pretend not to smell.

-Loretta Diane Walker

Be Still

Empty whispers in bated breath
forming wisps of life in air
did I breathe lonely close to death
half awake half dreaming in anxious despair.

Dream. Be still.

In the haze of the abandoned damp alley
stench of fear crawled, crept from gutters deep
friendly they came, all dressed to shout and rally
between the devil and angel my time to keep.

Listen. Be still.

Flashes of childhood, days of blazing glory
sweet nothing on swings and walls
wistful love and heartbreaks, my precious story
running through the doors and study halls.

Ache. Be still.

Gushing with pride, adorned with medals galore
courage and fear on a battlefield roll
never was it enough, Life always wanted more
shot in a dark causeway death rings my knoll.

Pride. Be still.

When they find me, I will be history
never stood a chance to say goodbye
pointlessly mugged, my death a passing mystery
left struggling, gasping, bleeding I slowly die.

Dead. Now still.

-Sandhya Suri

(The fragility of life is full of experiences and moments of utter vulnerability and insane courage. Most days it is a journey of actualization that one is a soul on Earth for the human experience. There are only two constants in life that make up the sum total of our existence; change and death. Everything in between has been placed to engage your soul in that human experience that the soul needs to understand the transient nature of the world, to make the best of it and believe in the stillness we are blessed with in little breaks until the final stillness.)

Light has no Shadow

Melting, my heart whimpered
candle wax, to the sides weeping
flickering in the lull of the night
love unrequited, mine now for keeping.

The salt of my tears warm, they taste of dreams
mirage and reality thins out the line;
what the truth was, isn't now holding good
his truth, the truth and that which is mine.

Darkness gnaws, creeping slowly into my soul
dance little shadows mocking my life,
flickering in the candles' fickle device
dipped in blood, reckless, I still hold the knife.

Wait! I pause, and a light breaks, warming my soul
those were just my shadows I saw on the wall
it occurred to me then, I could live again
light has no shadow and I need not fall.

-Sandhya Suri

(In the depths of our darkness we become our own light. It takes looking within, absorbing what's in the now and actualizing a life yet to be. Hope comes from darkness and light, when you begin to understand the shadows.)

what the fuck

I pause at some God forsaken space
the poems frozen, winter lakes
in the peak of summer breeze
tiny alphabets blow everywhere
teasing and taunting but never quite gathering

sighs and tears, through it all it jeered
made a laughing stock of my feelings
those embarrassed tears ran amuck
gathering What the Fucks over and over
until the supply seemed to break a wall
digging holes into aspirations
giving orgasms after orgasms
inside my head
the letters still aflutter

what the fuck

dammit! Won't you still yourself
I have tales to tell
the babies cry, insomnia plagues the mothers
lullabies hang on trees
dewdrops that grow in darkness
and laugh as they fall
another missed calling
another dusted night
announcing dawn

the lights are too bright
the font too small
the ideas too big
to fill my seasonal fall
come winter, won't you light a fire
the chimney stalls and chokes
ashes of despair softly in ashen dust
cover the pristine hopes of tomorrows

what the fuck
the pen runs dry
my mouth too
the throat is constricted
as undeniable truths of violent morons
assault my sensibilities

all I dream are of spaces far away
the ones I grew up with
Enid Blyton in that fancy font
and I, plucking fantasies
what the fuck is wrong with this world
that doesn't let people be
or animals that shimmer and fade
to extinction

the Earth laughs and evolves
for, we aren't far from it
the plastic chokes the soil
dusty are our throats
the cancer grows in spurts
and then with a slam dunk

the cookie crumbles in the milk
(contaminated in selfish agendas)
closed eyes come calling
insomnia and nightmares a sonata dance

what the fuck!

(whew)

-Sandhya Suri

(This particular piece is written keeping in mind our mindless abuse of the planet, our inner turmoil, the external uncontrollable things and the frustration of not being able to make a substantial difference.)

Zandunga

Me llaman Zandunga
como la canción favorita de Frida,
me gusta bailar,
soy una mujer llena de alegría,
rompo corazones al pasar,
tocan a mi puerta
pero no los dejo entrar,
me escriben canciones,
poemas y cartas,
soy música profunda,
de la que sabe amar,
de la de marimba,
no paro de cantar,
me llaman ingrata
cuando solo doy amistad,
soy buena amiga,
sé escuchar y consejos dar,
de cumplidos, soy agradecida,
cierro los ojos cuando no debo mirar,
soy única,
nunca perfecta,
simplemente soy auténtica,
soy de mi vida, arquitecta,
soy yo misma,
si a alguien le molesta
mi carisma
que se mueva,
que no estorbe mi caminar.
Seré Zandunga
hasta el final.

-Érika Elisa Garza Tamez

Humankind's Tribulation

Such affliction the world faces
with so many lives lost each day.
A horrific pandemic with no apparent
end in sight and our hope
begins to slowly diminish
if normality will once again
be regained with only the nostalgia
remaining of what once was.

We will never again take for granted
a loved one's warm embrace
or being able to go anywhere
without our face partly covered
for the greater good and to
prevent even more mortalities.

We come to learn how important trust is
as we witness many people afraid
of accepting a vaccine the government
and health experts strongly recommend.
Unbelievably, despite of the facts and
great loss of life witnessed worldwide,
many still believe the virus is all a hoax.

Yet, my faith is unyielding that this tribulation
the entire world faces together
will soon come to an end
where we will all rejoice once we prevail
and annihilate this heinous virus

that may have halted our lives
but failed to kill the invincible spirit
that defines all humankind.

-Vanessa Caraveo

Decanting dance

Waiting is searching,
searching suddenly,
the woman understands something
for which she had not searched.

Out comes the light
to place everything within brackets,
to shape that
which she ever needed.

Wounded queen,
cycle of remarks,
tell who I was,
who I am.
Around in circles the clay spins
and ends up where it began.

Flowing leaves,
mother-of-pearl buttons,
land of no miracles
craving for water.

Woman,
pour from the amphora
and dance
upon the solitary plain.

-Joselin Mejia Garcia

September

It's been a year since my heart broke beyond repair.

Still, the hole soars deep, like a never-ending bottomless pit.

I'm freefalling…

Spiraling, spinning, and spinning…

A silver slice of a shattered moon

shooting down to earth with no place to land, out of control.

That September day… a nightmare, I continue to live

over and over in my mind hoping the outcome paints change.

Like a paragraph in a horror novel, I read the same words in a loop, stuck.

Why, my beautiful mommy?

Why? Love— I thought I knew.

Now your unconditional love lingers beyond touch.

My sun spills empty, crying unknown tears.

"Everyone has their set time," you said.

How did you know? How could you have known?

I sit, staring at the endless eternity— and wonder as I absorb your smile in my mind.

I hear your tender voice in the blazing red cardinal singing hello at my windowsill.

Oh! As the white Calla Lilies I planted by the patio last spring dance with you in the wind,

the sun smiles in golden rainbows.

I sense you in my beautiful grandbaby's silky smooth skin as she jumps for joy,

wrapping her tiny arms around my neck.

You're in my words as I type everything on my laptop, key after key.

You're in my tears caught in my throat with every magnified memory,

like the dew on a rose's petal after the break of dawn slowly rolling off my chin;

joining its fate among the rest… bouncing off the floor no challenge for the crumpled tissue.

You're in the ceilings and walls of our home, still holding your floral scent

and in the cracks of the kitchen linoleum floor, tingling my toes.

Why? Sweet, Mommy, why?

Why did it have to be your set time?

-Sylvia Sánchez Garza

Awaken!

Awaken!
Your glowing, golden eyes
Illuminate beyond…
Pouring hearts from the rainbows

Wherever you go
The sun smiles, sprinkling tiny fragments
Oh, the moon smiles back—
Shine on eternal beauty

Wherever you exist
Your golden eyes glow forever
Iridescent through eternity
Through the opaque veil…

Sneaking a peek
Of angelic spirits
Going about their everyday lives
Soaring, spinning, singing their la la la's

As the bead of an iridescent tear
Splashes salt onto the green earth
And love and life blends into
Chaos and struggles in-between blurred worlds

In your mind…
The words overflow
Like faucets with broken handles
But from your mouth,

Silence—
Blocked lumps in your throat burn
Through to your stomach
A bottomless pit extinguishes
But does not crush,

For you know, those precious lost words
Will ignite and explode
In their own time, even if just
In your mind

-Sylvia Sánchez Garza

I dreamt that a sea wave

I dreamt that a sea wave
dragged me to you,

the blue
fills me up inside

with the promise of replacing your
warmth.

I submerge into my childhood— a sad substitute for the
feeling of breathing again,

the image of my broken body
still haunts my dreams,

and the memory of always being lost makes a home
inside me.

I saw your eyes today when my lungs were filled
up with water.

I saw your eyes today when the sky
was silent.

I saw your eyes today and your voice echoed
through my ribs.

I promise you, next time, I will not be a
drowning leaf, but a ship instead.

I promise you, next time, I will
replenish the sea with images of you.

-Sandra Dolores Gómez-Amador

She

She is an artist. She wants you in moments, thin skinned and bird-boned, she wants you when the shadows dissipate, and your lips are ripe with promise

She is a poet, she wants you in tragedy, she wants your belly fat with lucid smoke, impervious to the inevitable loss of identity, she wants you in paragraphs and by-lines

She is a singer, she wants your obsession, she wants you in velvet chairs and stoic silence, she wants your wine glasses and nimble fingers

And I ask: Is this how you want me?

She ashes her cigarette on my mother's sofa. She wants me in the sparks, fading on the cracked leather.

-Jules Schulman

Heaven is in the Water

Heaven is in the water, Bubba Fran sang to me.
Her mother didn't care for beaches much; She'd find God in other things:
The cracked porcelain set she had bought from a Kupiec for a lock of her hair,
The triangular mezuzah marooned on the basement floor. *What would the neighbors think if they knew a Jew lived here?*
The alkaline scent of bleach on her scalp, erasing the Egypt from her roots.
The letters to her father, shattered English phrases, mixed with lyrical Polish poetry
Water reminded her of home: the pregnant silence of Elk Lake in January,
Her landlord's cat offering furballs and dead rats in exchange for a cup of milk,
The deli man who delivered smoked kielbasy with kraut every evening like a prayer.
The death that coated the air.
After that month in 1939, they all smelt like it, cloying and heady. She'd bathed her daughter twice a day. Bubba Fran had loved the water.

-Jules Schulman

The Affiliate of Memory

Die is cast, thrown and tumbled
woman is born a girl, girl is born a woman
when she is young, learning to tie bows in sensible brown shoes
spit and shine, tighten pigtail, don't get your bobby socks dirty
what does she know of her future?
when then, what hour marks, her turning, her awareness?
the tempura fragility of her succulent heart
will she be like her grandmother, a blubbering mess?
able to condone slithered evil in the hands of her husband?
look the other way, for her choices are meager
will she be like her mother, a loyal lover?
seeking a man willing to hold her closer to the sun
melt Icarus, melt, till you can stand the radiance no longer

In that wicked knowing when after-birth is dried and shell chewed to starlight
she stands tall and unversed like a question mark, when she wants to scream out;
whydontyoufeellikeido?
she's the burnt slice of toast grown cold on countertop
everyone else is easy in the sun like white wheat and blackcurrant
children thread their way through oboe chair-backs like grass snakes
meadow flowers droop in her sweaty palm
she'd gift her indigo heart if it were taken or sensical
learning many years ago, don't lend, what you can't live without
she has enough air to fake it for fifteen minutes, then she's out
caught in the idling headlamps of smoky cars
no destination, just drive far to escape those pitch eyes, drained of regard
the ease with which you are in the loosening of your need, an affiliate of memory
put in glass jars along with sugar, watching you lean now, so evenly
toward tomorrow's sun

-Candice Louisa Daquin

Its Shining Water

Then make me a tree
that I may reach through earth, lengthening root
climb up, take form
gather again, that moment shook, from memory never
where moon was twice its natural size
reflected in your angry eyes
sitting in idling car
my sticky throated youth, your still punching vigor
movement then, as taught immemorial
of lovers who are not yet.
…
watchful of your thin wrist, flickering just before touch
warm air, window down
languid stroke of time, painting all these years hence
something you have absented from, like unpicked fruit
in turning, strange and unfamiliar

I dial that feeling quite often
not fantasy, no, something real painted over
turned to shellac, too hard to prize open again
…
I watch her in time
the girl I was, wondering at her thoughts
as I know them almost unformed and loose
the auburn xylophone of her back
I could fall in love with each of us again
the blush of your pomegranate lips

how your dark eyes soak up light, extinguish it black
no wonder, I say … no wonder
…
yet, would I be here now?
if I had not beseeched night in stolen lament;
if it is meant … let her call
a moment, as electric as fire burns oxygen
female silhouettes of trees sway in night breeze
would they have whispered?
no don't do it, don't go, turn back
heavy keys in light fabric, jingle like steps
wide open unrehearsed land rushing past
silence and folded roosting birds, holding their breath
…
it wasn't lust, it wasn't yet love, something other
we were always in between, time and sense
every song written about
when you leaned, close enough
fusion then, a kind of glory, unspoken of to this day
sealing our fate like flightless coin run over many times
shall silver in tarmac, make an echo of the very stars
blessing its shining watch

-Candice Louisa Daquin

Period

Thumbs drag white cotton to tile   splashes from a sea unknown plead down two virgin legs   heat climbs up to eyes wishing stains blur away   experience came before knowledge   she sits still on the cool seat curious now little fingers glide down to the spot untouched feels a warm wet wild oozing red and brown frosting unlike any sweet cake swiftly   call for reinforcements and mother comes to give the secret wrapped in a box about the journey   to womanhood to breasts to lovers to reoccurring pain   this gift she must keep until it is taken away just as quickly as it came.

-Kara Hollowell

Desalojo

De pie frente al espejo sólo
puedo ver
una casa encantada,

sus ventanas están rotas, las
puertas incompletas,

y todas las pequeñas habitaciones dentro de ella
están habitadas por la imagen de ti.

Recientemente he comenzado a pensar
que vivo a partir de recuerdos
que no me pertenecen,

fotografías amarillentas, periódicos del día de mañana,
el vacío que dejaste en la parte inferior de mi columna,

esa brisa fría:
una remembranza del día
en el que partiste.

Tal vez este cuerpo
no es más que los estragos de la inundación,
un dolor profano en la vértebra abandonada
de esta ciudad.

-Sandra Dolores Gómez-Amador

Eviction

I stand in front of this old mirror and
all I can see
is a haunted house,

its windows are broken, the
doors are crooked,

and all the small rooms inside it
are inhabited by the image of you.

I have thought for some time now
that maybe I am living through memories
that do not belong to me,

old pictures, tomorrow's newspaper,
the emptiness you left in the small of my back,

that cold breeze— a
remembrance of the day
you left.

Perhaps this body
is no other than the havoc of the flood,
a profane pain in the abandoned bones
of this city.

-Sandra Dolores Gómez-Amador

I Sing My Death Song

What do you know about Hell
Until you've buried a son under the desert floor
Rage and the Texas heat searing the skin on your neck
I've dwelled with the withering souls
Wandering Comanchería on a black horse
Haunting the dusty roads
Dying slowly
Slowly being reborn
Death has a trigger
Six keys to the underworld primed in a spinning cylinder
Half a dozen roads to travel to avenge my name
Love is a lie
Lie down and die
After you've paid your debts with blood and lead
Pain is my ally
Anguish my friend
They remind me of you
Unsettled scores
The Red River runs wild
Surging with Comanche blood
I came north to die
To curse the stars down from the sky
And lie
Face down in burned yellow grass
To heave off all this pain
Bullets split, splintered through my heart and brain
Let my life seep into the cracked earth
You've said your goodbyes
Kisses from the tip of a scorpion's tale
In the desert I sing my death song

-David Place

I Was a Wild Thing

I - was a crying thing
Howling drunk with the dogs
I - was a dying thing
Nosing in the dirt for a mouthful of worms
I - was a lying thing
Telling my heart that it could never be loved
In Gehenna
Demon-loving kings offer up their sons
Feeding innocence to fanged, bloodthirsty things
There, I learned the fire of the searing sands
Cloaked deceivers stole him away from me
Yellow pits of smoldering brimstone
Horned gods reveled in triumph
Celebrating over my suffering soul
Disciples of Moloch
Supplicants of Baal
God Damn you and your devils
You supplanted my name
As father
From his lips
Carried him off
To be raised by a witch
Godless
Nameless
Bastard
Orphan
Slow death
This heartbreak
The blood draining from my veins
The absence of a child

-David Place

On the Altar of Athena

Punish her Athena
Punish her
For tempting me
Punish her
For being so beautiful
To make me come
From the bottom of the sea
With slithering things
I crept up the temple stairs
Tentacled, crawling things
Dreams
Black and powerful as nightmares
From the door I watched her
Pulling the stars down from her hair
I came on her in your temple
White capped waves
Rhythmic raging
Cry out
Beneath the lord of the deep
In awe she trembled and shook
I - am the god of the sea
In pain she quaked and broke
I - am the god of the sea
I left her open on your altar
Sea foam sticky on her breasts
I left her wet upon your altar
Green streaks of algae spread across her legs
Crabs pinching on her flesh
Punish her Athena—for luring me
I - am the god of the sea

-David Place

Language

Language.
A mother tongue with a father spirit.
Color.
The notion that I should always know my place.
Nicknames:
Mi amor, Mi reina, Mi vida, spic, wetback, beaner
Go back to where you belong. Go BACK to where you belong. Go back to where YOU belong.
To be Latin. Is to have no identity.
From the moment I was born, I was every woman.
A bridge between opportunity and oppression.
But when a little girl that is every woman tries to be her own
She can't. She doesn't know how.
I was a wild child, never had a bloody nose nor
Broken bone yet the parts of my brain are left with this
Red kind of stain.
Back to WHERE you belong. Go back. You.
Ni de aqui, ni de alla. I'll never know my ancestors, yet their blood will stay with me forever.
The forever home filled with suffering, pain, hope, and dreams.
I never talk from comfort only to provide it for another
To know two languages is a blessing and a curse. To have pride to stand between a border.
This is home grown love. I am latina, africana, francés, indigena, árabe, italiana, y mucho más.

Nanti, mother. The ground.
Tata, father. My name.
A woman who can conquer not through division, but through unity.
She is neither black nor white, because she is not that simple.
She is the color of cafe con crema, she is the color of wheat, she is us.
She is our name. She is the unity that can bring together nations. She is every woman.
She is herself, she is here and
She is not going anywhere.

-Julie Matta

⌘ About the Author

about her: beacon persistent
manifestor of previously uncrossed stars
puller down of such cosmos

voice of the voiceless
undaunted historian of human striving
protest sign in poems held up against systems
breaker of systems

the poet is the breaker of systems
the poet is the builder of new systems, worlds

perhaps she is from those other worlds, here, in fact,
on sabbatical from stint as stardust
walking in human feet
for a cycle of orbits that has no language here

life on earth is a practice in darkness
overcoming
the poet speaks the language of overcoming

she is, too,

wife of master naturalist so de facto master naturalist
leaf inspector, bloom herald, bird singer
onto page
holder of light against all things
seemingly heretofore
opaque

-Kai Coggin

⌘ I Find My 2020 Glasses from New Years

I find my 2020 glasses from New Years—
silver and plastic, they tumble out of the art closet

to the floor, their tangible irony hangs at my ankles.
I pick them up, move them in my hands (shiny, unthreatening),

slip them onto my face this icy December full moon night,
look back through the lens-less lenses, cold curious senses,

to see what I can see, to look back on this year that's changed us all,
and the last time I wore these glasses, I wished for clarity,

but I didn't mean it like this, I didn't mean 2020 perfect vision
making everything that mattered suddenly come into blinding focus,

I blink & 2020 floods the backs of my eyes, reckless & cruel,
the reflective mirror sheen infinities me into flashback loops,

a gold star diagonals my left eye & the zeroes open eye holes,
the first 2 juts my right cheekbone & the other 2 bridges my nose,

a year spelled out on my face, spelled out on all our faces in the letters
of the lost, the sounds of their names, the holes we heavy—

& maybe there is symbolism in the positioning of these signs,
cheap drugstore party favor turned crystal ball visionary rhymes,

& I have tried to come to this poem from all possible sides,
wanted to mark this year with something meaningful that I write,

but the words just don't come, no matter the hum of my brain turning
over the days in my hands, I'm numb, I breathe, I breathe again—

I pain over the lines, & sometimes a poem can't paper cup oceans,
or see the clarity in 2020 glasses at the end of this darkest year,

trying to pen some clever flip of a script none of us knew the words to,
year that cut us off at the knees, made us grieve, & question our beliefs,

these frames that name all the pain & growth we've blamed on a year
that dropped all the balls on us, dumpster-fire-hell-scape we called living,

the socially-distant-my-god-I miss-you-please-don't-die we called surviving
& all I can think of is 2020's grand design began with wildfires,

over a billion animals in Australia burnt to bushland black,
devastation starting in the animal kingdom, their spirits phoenixing,

I taught a poetry class to children here, while children there cried
under red apocalypse skies & I wrote a poem— "Koala in Past Tense"

should've dedicated it us, precursor to a year of staring down tenses,
becoming present, becoming past, hoping desperately for a future,

& the clues were forming in the fiery atmosphere, every paradigm
we knew was about to go up in flames, singe & wither, fall away,

then Kobe crashed into a mountainside, died on a January day, he was 41.
I turn 41 in two days & I see the shock wave of one man's death,

& how one death seems to carry more weight than 339,000 in the tonnage
of grief, but how do I quantify something like that in a poem?

This is January, was January in the year of our lord oh lord what now,
& a billion animals hovering in the ethers saying wait humans,

your kingdom comes & the plastic glasses on my face heavy
with each memory, slide into the cold of February & the first death

from COVID finds our shores, impeached president resident demagogue retains
his rei(g)ns on darkness & we go on in our untouchable americanness

thinking this virus is only in otherlands, the autopilot of our lives about
to grind into a halted March. We watch Italians lock down, sing operas

from aching balconies, waters of Venice clear from lack of humans,
dolphins swim, & by Friday March 13th, I am hiding in a bathroom

in an elementary school between classes, waiting in fear of children's hands,
waiting for the school to shut down, then everything shuts down, locks
down & we mouthed the words global pandemic for the first time.
Breonna Taylor was also shot that day, look how the storylines coincide.

We lose half our faces behind masks, scrub-scald our hands raw, wipe
down groceries, collectively hold breaths, as daily the deaths take us, take us.

April we shelter in place, howl every night for essential workers, clap
for the heroes, bang pots from balconies, & New York City piles with bodybags.

There is not enough space to bury all the dead, this pervading image
runs through my head, still peering through these 2020 eyes in dread.

May, mayday mayday we're crashing crashing, we can't breathe,
I CAN'T BREATHE George Floyd screams, neck under knee of brutality,

May, in masks we take to the streets, two pandemics— COVID-19
& Black men historically being murdered by police, BLACK LIVES MATTER we
shout

& hold protest signs, I see thousands march in this poetic rewind,
& in May we crossed over an unfathomable number— 100,000 dead

as science naysayers & redhats pool party for memorial day instead,
the peoples' divide widens, the 2020 glasses crack down the bridge,

June we topple confederates, battle literal nazis as tensions rise,
thousands more die, July & August summer of our own wildfires,

If only we swept the forest of dead leaves trump said, & it is what it is
when talking about the Americans dead, & there is a hope that rises

in the back of our masked throats, in a few months we'll all rise to vote
in the most influential election of our lives, but from August to November,

we still have to survive, John Lewis and RBG cross over to fight
from the other side, trump tells the proud boys to stand back & stand by,

& this reel to reel remembrance through 2020 party favor glasses
can't lose focus now, must see it all, can't lose the vision that

the division between those of us who believe in science & those
who balked at COVID compliance, drove us only further into graves,

another hundred thousand lives could've been saved, they said
goodbye to their families on iPads, choked on ventilators in ICU,

this was summer's other narrative, the untouchable deaths & what
loneliness can do, & how we all became pixelated bodies on zoom

reaching out reaching out as we humans do. Let's skip to hope now,
the election won, vaccines, the words light & tunnel, the dark winter

blooming into possible spring & I can see clearly now,
my 2020 perfect vision blurred with tears of everything lost,

but look at what we have gained. Paradigm shifts rippling through
all of humanity take disaster & sometimes calamity, take breaking

& reshaping, dust returning to dust, fires burning everything
all at once, & maybe you found out what really matters this year.

Maybe all of us who survived & are still surviving, will have
the eyes to see, will have the hearts to heal, will have common

struggle & stories, just like in putting on these 2020 New Year's
glasses & remembering this painful glorious year, I see

that everything that mattered was already in front of me,
I married the woman I love, I wrote poetry, I fought like hell

for American democracy, I put my hands into the soil &
we ate vegetables planted from seed, I learned to identify

birdsongs singing from the trees, I stretched & I stretched

into a higher version of me, & this was the gift of 2020.

You see, clarity comes in many forms. All of us, all at once
had the chance to see things more clearly, to hold closer

to our hearts what we really hold dearly, to learn and work
beside our growing children, to shape our own little worlds rebuilding.

I will keep this vision always, place the 2020 glasses on
my office bookshelf, remember the perceptions gained,
the higher insight suddenly ordained, the clarity of crystals
glimmering like stars in my eyes, guiding us all perhaps

to a better home, a better world,
on the other side of this year we survived.

-Kai Coggin

⌘ My Whole Soul Is In It
(for the poets in the resistance)

"To heal, we must remember."
- The 46th President of the United States, Joseph R. Biden

It's already like a war story
in my mouth, making it to this moment,
the shrapnel embedded in our hearts still gleaming
with fresh wounds, and it is the morning
and trump is gone, riding still the tails
of his atrocities turned so-called wins,
tooting still his own sad little horn
even in the final moments
of his jilted departure,
"have a nice life"
he says, and you know what?
I will now,
we will now,
for it is morning,
it is *this* morning in America
we are awake and the sun is rising
after a four year nightmare,
and we don't want to remember.

"To heal, we must remember."

We don't want to remember all that unfolded
during the demoralizing trump regime,
the times we cried and lost hope,
how we forgot to dream,
but we've written it all into poems, haven't we?
Took it upon our tender hearts to chronicle the chaos,
like some weary scribes of human history,
like in the future some sentient beings will stumble

across our defiant light slivered in the darkness,
and say *here— there were poets with words
holding evil to the fire.*

To heal, I remember my own catalog
of *American carnage.*
Grab them by the pussy, a poem,
the Muslim ban, a poem,
Paris Accord withdrawal, a poem,
un-shaping glaciers, I wrote a poem,
very good people on both sides, another poem,
children in cages, a poem and a foil blanket
worn like a cape, leading a protest,
transgender military ban, a poem,
north korean nuclear face off, a poem,
the border wall, the hate, the nazis, poem poem poem,
school shootings and lockdown drills, poems,
another black boy dead,
another
another
another
another—
pandemic, poems, so many poems.
      I wouldn't write a poem for the insurrection,
      I wouldn't bend my words that low.

Every day, every lie, every new fresh hell,
the rancor and violence, the taste and the smell,
and I never went poem numb from his callous (un)heart,
saw myself in the constant mode of fight or flight,
stomach tight, waiting for the next gut punch,
jaw grinding the names of the dead in my teeth,
and poetry was the only sword I had that felt right,
letters strung together to form a vibration of light.

Love poems and nature poems too,
but naming his atrocities always bleeding through.

And it is morning now,
on the day of all our Lords, January 20, 2021,
and just for today, we can put down our swords,
the vacuous stain has been airlifted to *I don't really care where*,
and the sun is steadily rising over the reflection pool
shining over pillars of light that mark the 400,000 we've lost,
compassion and empathy made their first stop here last night,
the first act of this new administration touching down in DC
was to remember our dead, to grieve and to reflect,
to remind us we are still whole in our humanness,
fragile in our loss,
stronger together in our hope,
and a Black covid nurse sang *Amazing Grace*
like an angel,
and I wept at the beauty,
I wept for the return of our hearts,
the reflection of us in light shining into this morning,
this mourning, with a u, mourning with you,
the inverted mirror of backwards chaos upside-down everything
flipping back into the real, and a bird outside my window
is trumpeting a herald song, and it is morning,
and in America this morning, finally, I feel like I belong.

"To heal, we must remember"

Poets, we can look into our minds
and remember each line written into the library
of consciousness, scribbled in the dark
into the book of now,
our words running together
to form a criss-crossing network of the real peoples' history,
the true colors of our sorrow and joy,

and this morning I am ready
to burn it all into a new fire,
make it into a star
of *let's never get this close*
to destroying ourselves again.

I am ready to undocument the night
of its chaos, of its pain, I am ready
to write about hope and beauty again,
to fill all the white space with color,
stop the enjambments so we are all in line together,
walking toward a tomorrow where we are all on the same page.

Let this poem be my last reflection of that old country,
the inverted mirror we lost ourselves in
and found ourselves in again dressed as votes,
dressed as love and inextinguishable hope,
and this morning, a new chapter of our story begins,
we wake up with shattered ceilings under our feet
the glass on the ground and in our hair
shimmering like the cosmos fell,
it will be soft, not sharp,
it will sing and hum in the song of becoming sky,
and today in America
a Black South Asian woman
(all women) will RISE.

I am an American flag
on that distant inaugural lawn,
my stars and stripes waving
like a prayer and a poem in the winds of change
my colors of reclaimed red, white, and blue
shine with new and vibrant hues,
and this is my country again, my god,
this is our country again.

On this hard fought Inauguration Day,
after I sing and cry and dance distant with all of you,
after the reality of change sinks into my bones,
and my tears of hope wash my spirit new,
I will roll up my sleeves, America—
we have work to do

    and my whole Soul is in it.

-Kai Coggin

Something, Ending

"*God is gender free.*" Amalia Ortiz

"*I can't breathe, mama, mama*" he calls out.
anima mundi, universal soul has answered
with planetary wounds,
marks on our own hands & feet.

Now Let Us Shift

Prometheus Corona
Her crown draped with a face mask
will not save, condone or condemn us.

We move to save earth
from ourselves,
bring fire to the night—birth seeds
foreshadow the darkest of the earth to shine Black.

The maguey blooms, and its muscles droop,
sculptural leaves evaporate,
give water-life to the blossoms, then black seeds,
and to the tangle of pups, babies growing at her base.

We/they had it wrong with light white supremacy
We are blinded like the man, on the road to kill.
Sight returns on the third day, with dusk.

I am the other you
You are the other me.

We are not separate,
but YinYang, enjoined-- silverized
by beating, pumping, breathing.
Shiva, Hapi, Great Manitou

Energy is motion
and then in rest.

-Kamala Platt

Egrets' Elegies
After Derek Walcott

Winter of Westside Displacement

First week of Advent, city workers don white hazmat suits,
prefiguring the prevalence of pandemic protective garb.
Men board motorboats and rafts, journey out,
and with the slow, deliberate fury
of a 21st Century cyclone, they make landfall,
deboard on Bird Island. Stirred by Avian phobias
they stomp out and bag the vegetation in devilish pantomime.
By the beginning of Halcyon Days,
they have denuded Bird Island.

Following city edicts, men in suits remove all nests.
Audubon volunteers transfer six nests south of town,
rewire them into trees on the banks of recycled sewage waters
where people visit from the northside
and other waterfowl abound.

In the interim, westside barrio displacement threatens
Alazán-Apache, Los Courts, built, 1937.
Plans are set in place for generations of birds and people
who share decades, neighborhoods, la paz en el barrio,
to be sent packing.

One sunny afternoon, two Great Egrets
venture out on the island's barren ground;

they arch wings and dance, rising in rhythm
each with the other, dance to drumbeats
we cannot hear.

Their dance defies the city
that denies them roost and nest.

They dance a final dance, fly off,
follow waters to the Gulf.

-Kamala Platt

A Love Like That

I was told by my brother to transcribe your life
Record your voice and write a book and leave it for
the children I would never have

And several Thanksgivings ago we tried,
your memories stuck in a loop:
The importance of education
The army
And World War II
Not making way for what came between
Then and marrying mom

But you did tell your stories not meant for us
In meeting after meeting after you took your
Last drink more than 50 years ago
Stories that belonged to a man we never knew

But traces of that man still remained
until you took your last breath
Because you told my mom never to wake you by touch
And I still remember the sound of your nightmares

But I also remember hearing her laughing,
you had come up behind her,
turned her gently in a kiss while she made dinner

I wonder how a love like that is captured

-Linda F. Romero

Four wishes

There exist candles that never go out,
Where the weeping wax never ends.
They flicker shadows in the solace, soul of the beat,
And brighten them to a fading wave.

Where the weeping wax empowers,
Is where I rock you in my arms,
And frighten the shadows to a fading wave,
Enough to make life bearable.

Is where I rock you in my arms
A dream or my imagination?
Enough, this life's unbearable,
And four wishes stand on your birthday cake.

A dream and my imagination,
Flicker in the solace, soul of my beat.
Four wishes on your birthday cake,
But there exist candles that never go out.

-Mark Esperanza

She, too - *Inspired by "I, too" - Langston Hughes*

Born in Mexico and arriving in America at age eleven,
Mother only knew the language of her nation.
And she held on to them long after learning English.
Her words mythologized the mountainous region of Zacatecas.
The caves and valleys and ravines
and people with ancient languages and ancient homes.
And she wrote about the golden cathedrals
where priests talk closest to God. There were pyramids too. Pyramids that spoke in ancient tongues and held ancient
people with ancient prayers.
And when the memory of her city faded,
she wrote of otherness into a white-feathered notebook.
Placed on a pedestal,
America sang to her.
The light brown girl with birdlike carols,
sang with the brushing rhythm of a broom.
Sang with the stirring bowl of flour and the rolling
of a pin to compress dough into tortillas, into tacos with too much beans.
Sang lovely lullabies to a baby brother and sang low when he passed away.
She sang with happiness too.
Sang with the bosses of Edcouch- Elsa ranches, before they fled after the '68 walkout.
She sang too in the kitchen, like others before, but without the laughter.
Sang in solace because she knew too America would see her beauty.

-Mark Esperanza

Knox and Henderson Streets

Last time I was there I didn't even recognize it

still just blindfold me and I could find where the Jersey Lily used to be

where they dared me to kiss the bartender

I leaned quickly over the beer mugs

then realized he kissed so many girls that his lips were dull

but the night was soaked in laughter and I was seventeen and on my

own in the city with twenty bucks in my pocket so who gives a flying fuck

it was cold but I had that sheepskin coat my uncle gave me and the best bell bottoms

platform shoes that made my legs want to dance and toes so happy

to be back in Texas after that cold Missouri winter the year before

this was a city I could grow to my own in, in a place where I could paint

write poems dream big as the sky talk my true thoughts

and we all loved rock n roll at the end of the night

I was so in love with my wooden chair curved, simple and elegant

Like the new life I owned I hugged it tight within my sheepskin coat

Braced myself became the new beast I chose to be

Walked right out the door and took it home

It's lasted longer than any kiss or man fits me still like a favorite paintbrush

Sayin' this is you girl this is where you belong

Let your love for yourself be the strongest

-Noël Bella Merriam

Aprons

Standing beside her in the kitchen each afternoon

formica kitchen counter speckled with gold stars spinning in electric light

white ruffled curtains edged with dark green rick rack

familiar smells of arroz con pollo onions and bell pepper sizzling soft

top of my head coming just up to her waist where an apron was tied

careful careful the stove is hot glowing pink in the late day's sunlight

quick hug as she lowered fresh plantains into another skillet

their perfect golden crust bursting open in my mouth at every dinner

after school she taught me to sew I perched at her dressing table

careful not to knock over the jungle gardenia maja coty face powder

unaware that I would always have to leave something behind

what I fear leaving behind now remembering her the sound of her voice

her long black hair kindness of her eyes intelligence soft laugh

this grandmother the only one with patience for me at six taking me in

teaching me to make my stitches as tiny as possible nearly invisible

my needle's silver point picking its way between individual threads of organza

edging my own tiny apron with eyelet lace to put a ribbon through she said

but I could never pick the perfect color left the lace white pure and untouched

an open web of memories drifting in and out

-Noël Bella Merriam

Lunada

Why would the moon need me?
She has her orbit and I have mine.
Yet there comes her call
As we light a fire with torches
Chanting her name in a thousand
Songs and as many tongues

Embers die as the bonfire passes
Over talk of the past and the lost
Yet the moon throwing her light over all
Echoing girlish voices from somewhere past,
"I see the moon and the moon sees me."
So she binds this night to nights gone by
When others lit their fires on their own hills
And sang in their thousand tongues:

Always, my sister
As long as you rise
Heavy with the night's promise,
Illuminate us and call.
We will come.

-Stan Raines

How do we explain the harm

There seems no need to return to this world
of steps flabbergasted rotations on the same
axis—you
the oldest living civilization on Earth loaded with
so much physical gasp like limes duly sliced I'm
not offended to be serious about sex, except we
know only the far end of it, not the part it must be
difficult to witness
plucking chrysanthemums yet finding no words
at the heart of me —you ask what is the ultimate
wind? *qi* is like water and words are
like objects floating on water.

-Moriana Delgado

Closed Eye Visuals

Prayers and trumpet tones
From somewhere out, beyond
The painted walls that hold my life
Wake me in false-dawn light of early May

And it is warm
Last winter's frost and snow
Receding into unforgotten
Stories told while drinking

Strobe flashes like fireworks
Outside the courthouse, closed eye visuals
Shipwreck current privacy of reason
Baked and seasoned

Cyclone syndrome skips the generations
That deny it
Dizzy Gillespie, high on speed
And blowing through his smile

Beer can ashtray
Red wood picnic table wet with garden spray
And houseflies
Make a home for open eyed sobriety

-PW Covington

Circular

Candy pixels seep into my bloodstream
Mainlined, like the Metro
Gondoliers steer through me, the astral me
The magnificent residue of my potential
Sensation stoned

What was wasted, always wasted
On the shiny things
And nights out on the edge of
The thin ice of fallacies and faith

Communion gin for half-rate sacramentals
Well-worn leather vestments, unpolished
Untouched tabernacles of disgust, decanted

I left it here, somewhere
That dreamscape nebula
That slipped through my screen door
On slipstream cigarette smoke, drifting

Through newspaper and poetry magazine
Deadlines, gin-pinched
In spite of all things circular,
Apocalypses rarely arrive on time

-PW Covington

The Custodians

for the forgotten custodians of our democracy

Who cleaned the Capitol of the mess that the mob made,
collected and tossed out discarded water bottles, bagged
and trashed spent spray cans and crushed cigarette butts?

Who swept the littered floors of the Rotunda and Crypt,
the Statuary and Speaker's office, brushed the remnants
of the shattered windows and broken benches into piles?

Who gathered the shards of glass and shreds of wood in
dustpans, emptied that trash in large black garbage bags,
then hauled the heavy receptacles to overfull dumpsters?

Who scrubbed the surfaces of that statuary, wiped clean
the patterned tile floors and dark smears of blood across
President Zachary Taylor's marble chin, lips, nose, eye?

Who checked the chambers and offices, closed up, then
cleared out of the Capitol, that secular sanctuary safe in
good care, cleansed of the stains of the disorderly horde?

-Jonathan Fletcher

Kentucky as Usual

At the derby, the thoroughbreds—chestnut, palomino, black,
gray, roan, brown, bridled in bit and headstall, take off at the
shot of a starter pistol in a race which lasts only two minutes.

Breonna Taylor lives past two minutes, even five or six yet
all the while alone and helpless, when officers fire 22 shots
through the window, then trample her apartment front door.

A quarter mile into the race, a blazed colt Authentic takes the
lead, remains a mere length and a quarter ahead of his nearest
rival, though in an upset wins with a finishing time of 2:00.61.

At 12:48 am, Breonna lies unresponsive in a pool of blood on
her hallway floor, where fellow emergency responders,
unable to resuscitate her, pronounce that young EMT dead.

Authentic, through his win, pays out to his bettors, $1.86 million
in all, and although that racehorse is awarded none of the money,
his name will be remembered, more than his owner's or jockey's.

Breonna's family is awarded a $12 million settlement,
none of which will ever bring her back, but like the bay colt
from the derby, her name's now a chant that nothing can trample

-Jonathan Fletcher

An American Tradition

On July 9th, 1776, upon hearing *The Declaration of Independence* read aloud for the first time, Washington and his troops charged the Bowling Green, where those patriots, moved by Jefferson's words to remove all gilded symbols of their oppression, hoisted ropes around a 4,000-pound statue of George III, mounted on horseback and robed like the Romans,

as they chanted: "Tear him down! Tear him down!"

They ripped from its base the garish monument that had long stood over them, smashed that cruel Crown to pieces and, in a most fitting reuse of that malleable material of subjugation for matériel, melted His Majesty down into 42,088 musket balls and then, through volleys of musket fire, returned the lead from that loathed likeness and won their independence.

-Jonathan Fletcher

Still it slumbers on

Turns out it was *because*.
All along.
Nothing else.
One defining word –
because
When tethered and withered and forlorn
and held
in the deep
it was a because
which blinded
and indentured us all
because
it is me and not them
because
they needed to teach us a lesson
because
the fate of the world beckons
because
the moral fabric demands it so
because
of my brown skin
because we exist
and thereafter the shallow followed
faithless as the seedling
yet
still, all along
and nonetheless
it was *because* which drowned us all

-M. Anthony Miranda

Flight of the Future Inmate

I hear one of us say
Ey
then the quaint and fateful calling of the bicycle warriors of the barrio
Vamos a tirar la vuelta.

And so
we ride down *Poblano Street*
then
down *Bicentennial Avenue*
the breeze at our heels
riding past the barking dogs beyond the mail-boxes and hurricane
fence-lines
America Boulevard near where Lupe lives
Republic Street where Raul's girlfriend stays with her tio and tia
then
Bevo's street
only
no one's there

His mom's Chevy ain't seen
and
so we treck down *Agostadero Street*
to where there's an end
then
the railroad tracks
and more tracks
y mas trakes
and
then
the sun shines down upon a new trail

another avenue left to explore
Otro barrio
anciano
y
distinto

We know the place
O, si, carnal, I hear the voice of my people call
sacred barrios untethered
and
left to be consumed

And so we ride
across the braided sky
and
we are one
and
I am here among them
with the height of the world calling me to go farther and further
so
we
and
phantom memories of liberation and Mando and Rudy and Bevo's
cousin Danny
we ride
and we are one
with the asphalt
and
the jangle of bicycle chains
and
the brake pedal at the ready

we live
and
breathe
and
we are one

-M. Anthony Miranda

FWB

Circled into a ball on the empty side of my bed
The blanket rests over my head
And loneliness peels into me
And creates a hole in my stomach
The few that kept me company for a moment
Distracted me from it all
Opened my thoughts to how soft things could be
I felt control
Stress relief shrouded in personal vanity
The end was signaled with a few pumps
Followed by the thickness of your heaving body
I lay crumbled under you
Dissatisfied
As you ask for water
One of three
One of four?
Did he know this would be the last time?
The fear of excitement dissipates when it is shallow
Empty
A hole cannot be filled with empty bodies
Will I soon know someone special?
Or will my couch be crowded with shapeless interactions?

-Kaitlin K. Howard

Christmas Eve

I lose focus thinking of you
My mind wanders to the touch of your hand
While I agree to disagree about facts with my mother
I divide my time between thoughts of you and the present
I hear the sound of you contemplating our next meal while I
Lift spoonfuls of macaroni into a plate
While nudging my sister's shoulder
I remember the smell of your underarm in the morning
Do you still play music to fall asleep?
As I close my eyes between conversations
I can see you laying on my chest
You would lift your head to look at me
And scoop me up in your arms as I cooked dinner
Will I ever be as excited with the gentle touch of a finger on my
shoulder?
Do you miss the secrets we kept
Or the closeness of our relationship, friend?
If I were younger I would let you spread me thin
Consume me until I was bare
It was always going to end

-Kaitlin K. Howard

Bone Dust

We cupped her velvet powder
Flecked with bone shards,
And paused in wonder and awe.

Then we flung her residue—
Her smile, her propensity to listen,
Her nervous twitch,
Her pluck, her "I'll be all right!"
Her "This, too, shall pass"— from the jetties.
Scoop-after-scoop, this dirt danced
With windblown froth.

Then, dust-filled gusts, doubling back,
Flung their contents, our mother's bones,
Onto our cheeks, foreheads, chins, noses!

And, amidst our grief, we chuckled,
As one does at absurdity,
This shock of intimacy,
This touching of bones—

An intimacy not unlike that of seeing her, our potent mother,
Like a tiny child, a silent comma atop white sheets,
Bald, except for a few hairs (liberated from chemo),
Sprouting like newborn leaflets.

Her powder curled and eddied
Down to sandy sediment.
And a hungry crab found sustenance,

And a hungry fish ate that crab.

Under her care, we thrived.
Now she, of gentle voice and soothing eyes,
May be the stuff of shark or dolphin—
She, whose velvet dust swept our faces.

-Kathy Trenfield Raines

Orchestrating Sons

Pointing to cellos, they swell mellow,
Violins soar in sun-dappled woods,
Timpani rumbles tigers,
Trumpets herald rescues,
Horns, a hunt,
Flutes, sprightly birds, chirp with glee!

Joy ensues as I direct.
Life slows to a worrisome minor adagio,
But resolves to a rollicking major rondo!
No missed notes, no squeaks, no malaise.

I know just what to do. I've practiced.
Why, I've even written the score.
Follow me, follow me.

But, each, smiling politely, writes his own concerto.

-Kathy Trenfield Raines

Unplayed Violin

You, yellowish brown, shiny and scarred,
Napping in a dark case beneath downy dust,
Await my courage, my time, my touch,
My patience and modesty.

Unplayed, untried, unchallenged,
Unstressed by fumbling, slowness,
Tension, history—wild, intent,
Searching for purpose in
You—innocent wooden receptacle—
You, who often yielded joy.

But you were pressed too hard
And ranked too high—
Too much responsibility for wood, steel and gut.
Like the Looney Toons frog—
The one who belted "Hello! Ma Baby" for his finder
But croaked "Ribbet!" for the talent scout—
We two only exulted alone.

We tensed. My fingers pressed the string too hard,
Making what my teacher dubbed my "buzzing bee vibrato",
While her plump fingers, as natural as mockingbirds,
Dropped onto the string and sang.
And, like wafting orange blossoms,
The sound astonished with sweetness.

Now you await our once innocent rejoicing.

-Kathy Trenfield Raines

Ventanas del alma

Ojos castaños,
Ojos tristes.
Ojos dulces,
Ojos profundos.
Ojos llenos de ternura
y caricias sedosas.

Ojos negros,
Ojos opacos.
Ojos repletos
de rabia y llanto.
Ojos de lobo solitario,
Ojos de condena y fervor.

Ojos lejanos,
Ojos gitanos.
Ojos que no sueltan
ni una lágrima de dolor.

"Te quise como a la niña
de mis propios ojos,"
despidiéndote me dijiste, mirándome a los ojos.

Llegó la noche sin luna,
y mis ojos siguieron
tus pasos.

Te fuiste, dejándome
con el recuerdo del imán de tus ojos:

Ojos castaños,
Ojos tristes,
Ojos lejanos, ventanas del alma.

-Maria Eugenia Trillo

Windows to the Soul

Sugar brown eyes,
Sad eyes.
Sweet eyes,
Profound eyes.
Eyes full of tenderness and
silky caress.

Black eyes,
Opaque eyes.
Eyes full
of rage and wailing.
Solitary wolf eyes,
Eyes of condemnation and fervor.

Eyes full of far-away spaces,
Gypsy eyes.
Eyes that don't shed
a single tear loaded with pain.

"I loved you like the apple of my eye",
you pronounced as you said goodbye,
looking me straight in the eye.

Night arrived without a moon,
and my eyes followed
your footsteps.

You left, leaving me
with the memory of
your magnetic eyes:
Sugar brown eyes,
Sad eyes,
Distant portals to the soul.

-Maria Eugenia Trillo

WHAT DOES A MAN SMELL LIKE?

A man smells like a man
of sawdust and piñon trees,
of mesquite burning in dark
saguaro desert air.

He smells of sun-kissed hair
and salty brine,
of water-tumbled rocks
of wounds never laid bare.

A man smells like a man
of windows thrown open
to prairie summer wheat-fields
of earth made damp with dew.

He smells of twinkling stars
and *kinnikinic* in his pipe,
of northern crisp, blue-green lights dancing on the black belly of
a pregnant winter night.

A man smells of incandescent bed sheets, of balmy wild currents
pungent with musky cinnamon, mandarins
and rum.

A man smells like fresh
full-brewed coffee,
curls of steam rising
to the yawning horizon.

A man simply smells
like a man.

-Maria Eugenia Trillo

Mariposa

Anaranjada, negra, blanca,
Volando, luciéndose, revisándose, pensando. Recuerda otra vida y se
pregunta, ¿qué es ésto? Metamorfósis.

Butterfly (translation of "Mariposa")

Orange, black, white,
Flying, showing off, looking herself over, thinking.
She remembers another life and asks herself, "What is this?" Metamorphosis.

-Maria Eugenia Trillo

Manual labor in a dress in exchange for a spicy chicken sandwich

Island Girl snores but Border Boy hasn't
told her yet. He can't find a way
to describe them without naming
a storm because all natural disasters feel
the same and she is lost
to the sea that doesn't show it wants
her, like Border Boy pulling away a little
too late to prevent collapse
in lungs steeled by salted air.

Border Boy doesn't know
how to properly cry, he shares,
when Island Girl helps him
move a mattress into his new place.
She drops it on her toes
and gets winded after a couple
steps. The number one
screwed next to his front
door is backwards in a way
that doesn't change anything.

They drop the mattress she will
never sleep on and he
sketches a future
that doesn't need her.
Bike rack next to the AC,
television in the dining room. What kind
of apartment has a dining room

but no bedroom doors? Maybe
the same kind that only has a lamp
and these two eating quesadillas on top
of cold tiles in a living room.

-Laura Andrea Vázquez López

Creation Myth Two: Holy Matrimony

The sun is out and it is raining.
It must be my wedding day.

A tiara of broken curls
shriek at my mother

doing my nails candy apple red
to make him kiss the ring, eat the ring

choke on stones more precious than I reflect. Refract the
sun on his insides.

When Mami said bruja
she didn't mean holy

but the cave-dwelling virgin brews rain to pair with a
freshly caught groom.

The sky was pretty once and so was I. He said so before I shat
his weight in gold.

Zero-sum on flowers, lace, and dirt all fake, cheap, and a
ritual over his grave.

Since brujeria is all in the hands, fingers, I swore fealty to
my claws,

a caricature of everything he milked from me. Spilled, spoiled, soured. Seared on the sky.

-Laura Andrea Vázquez López

What Mamá Gave

What is there to say when an outcome is the worst definition of some-
one seeing it all wrong,
  like a misinterpretation of love

in the brown paneled walls of a low-lit diner in your memory Where
strawberry sauce tastes like a petrochemical plant where who-being is
a fear, a silencing
  of what we might not deserve to have

and you can't put your finger on why, but it was a special place

When you spent time there with her
and you ate the terrible thing she ordered because you trusted, wanted
to make her happy
  because her unhappiness was the worst outcome of all

and not what she wanted for you,
but the sorrow she knew you learned from
  watching one-sided love she gave as daily duty

What she didn't want you to see, the afraid she might be, the
saids never meant, ones that should have, she
  choosing tongue-tied hollow over stuttering
and slipping words into hurt

She took all of that and shaped and formed, fortifying from her own
backbone, with her soft, beautiful, sometimes punishing hands, into
nothing significant that flipped her entire universe, and yours

So you'd know you deserve to have someday

          the strawberries that don't taste like plastic

-Kim Denning

Xōchipilli

Xōchipilli in stone,
my great grandfather in silvered emulsion,
soul of defiance snatched by photo
in downturned mouth,
eyes seeking eternity,
cheekbones reaching sky

Welcoming, posturing,
Come gringo,
take my land.

Your progress yields crops that burn in our vessels of clay

I entice you
with festivals and flower halos,
enrapturing you
in intoxicating bindings—
sunned skin,
tongue of gods,
vines imbued with provocation, and
Unconquerable *sangre fría*

Warmed to sludge,
my resins bear down,
forcing your feet,
casting off your trespassed loiter,
over time
through ancestral awakening
and feathered progeny

Xōchipilli haunts in altar'd smoke,
hummingbird warriors quicken in our mirrors,
waking to ofrendas
stained by limpias of fire, and
recuerdos dripping Mesoblood

-Kim Denning

Ready or Not

The staff lined up to say goodbye
their eyes trailing the taut, white sheet

lain over dried lips, a chest that won't rise
zipped in a heavy gray, plastic sac

their sad eyes eventually landed on mine.
Some gave hugs, more for them

I thought, held on too long, squeezed too tight but
now, the memory of faces, blurred

bodies, bestowing kindness, exuding warmth, life,
in his absence, yields a quiet refuge that rises and
falls

-Ritika Chand-Bergfeld

Queer Angst

Has
wishing away
blue weirdness
ever worked
for you
I wish
your worries could spin
pink silken skeins as light
and strong as gold gossamer
and attach itself
to the calm
dead sea and dissipate

-Ritika Chand-Bergfeld

Love of Land, Love of Man

In the foothills of the Himalayas
dreams are carried in incense-and-curry
filled air, the short distance to the heavens.
Fresh snowfall blankets the dung and trash heaps the lithe,
deodar pines and quaint homes with stone bases, wooden
arches and steeply pitched roofs.

I first met grandpa when I was 8,
in his cold blue concrete castle.
He demanded I finish my milk, served
warm and thick and reeked of goat. Did I
imagine it yellow? My stomach refused.
Grandpa grimaced, a scowl I recognized.

We met again, two decades later, same place this
time, greeted with his health records, he
commanded American answers, entitled,
his boys already turned to ash.
Conditional lover. I wept for mom,
and to discover how she became broken.

-Ritika Chand-Bergfeld

The Cat Has Passed On

from its lying down place
under the hedge, through
the receiving line
of neighborhood children,
taking its place
among the *ofrendas,*
calaveras y caléndulas,
on the *D´ıa de los Muertos*
Altar.

-Jeffrey L. Taylor

How to Survive the Family Curse

- **Intel**
  - Interview your mother, first of all, whose mind is still sharp
  - Obtain medical records (re: hospital stays, medication and dosages)
    - Anecdotes will suffice in a pinch
  - Cross-reference your strain against theirs; note the similarities and differences
  - Use or lose their survival strategies; what works for one may not work for another

- **Action Plan**
  - On your fridge, list the important numbers:
    - Suicide hotline
    - Best friend
    - Weed dealer
  - Hide notes for yourself in boxes, in the inside of cabinet doors, or your car.
    - Suggested phrases include, but are not limited to:
      - Smile. :)
      - Take your meds.
      - Your cat would miss you.
      - Have you called your friends lately?
  - Find a therapist in your city[1] or even online[2].
    - Note: not effective if you
      - Don't attend
      - Tune out their advice
      - Don't move on if their help isn't helping

- **Execution**
  - Hug your cat.
  - Open the window for as long as you can manage.
  - Take a shower.
  - Eat, even if it's frozen or takeout.
  - Remember that you are worth keeping alive.

-Tori Hicks

---

[1]https://www.psychologytoday.com/us/therapists

[2]https://www.betterhelp.com

Sometimes I Feel Things

I remember floating through the unknown astral plane with you.
The one that held us and cradled us close and dear.

I remember-

Surrounded by the energy of it.
Engulfed by the fire it birthed.

There was no pain.
There was no hurt.

The truth of it?
It lurked within us before our souls had ever met.

It's waves we rode separate into bliss,
colliding into liquid pleasure-
that dripped as one unto this world-
that is only you and I.

-Enedina Irene

They Do Not Know They Are Angry

Survival mode-
Can turn you into a well-oiled machine.

In many ways-
A warrior.

Not everyone will know your struggle.
Why would they?
Why would you want them to?

Sometimes the outside-
Does not always match within.
Sometimes-

If rage could blossom into a fire-
Could you see the beauty of the flame?

Lies!
You couldn't possibly-
Many people would be frightened.

And not understand-
What it is that they are witnessing.

Many would see an uncontrolled monster-
Whose value and beauty would mean more with death-
Than with breath.

No one tries to understand you when you are alive-
Only when you are no longer here-
So they could draw their own conclusion as to what led to the flame.

-Enedina Irene

Candied Silence

Your abuelo says he's going to the nursing home to see guelita.
So you go with him and you end up in some unfamiliar front yard,
Rickety fence, dirt, rocks, and a boy.

He's your cousin, you are told.
This is your tia. Give her a hug.
So you do because you are five.
She smells of drugstore roses and sour sweat.

They laugh and leave you with the boy,
Playing with dusty toy cars,
Sun singeing your pale skin,
Tossing rocks at empty soda cans,
Tummy rumbling for dinner.

They emerge from behind the rusty screen door.

Abuelo tucking his shirt.
Vamos a la tiendita, you are told.
We get you kendy.

So you are quiet on the drive home,
Hands covered in dirt and sticky, cherry flavored sweetness.
Mom asks if grandma liked the quilt she sent her.
Si, a ella le gusto, he says.

But you know she didn't see it because she was at the nursing home,

And grandpa wasn't there
And you played with an unknown boy
And hugged an unknown tia
And you are five
So you say nothing and choke down your candy.

-Valeka Cruz

Twirl

Twirl for me, he said   Dress floating in the afternoon sun
Swirls of pink and green flowers.
                                        I fell in a puddle

You are so pretty, he said   She giggled
in the warmth of the sun   Whirls and giggles and spinning blurs
                                        I ran through a sprinkler

Twirl faster, he said   A flash of white
eyelet trimmed panties   Dizzy giggles and spinning light
                                I jumped in a swimming pool

Pretty girls kiss boys, he said   Spinning
room and rough hands   Bubbling tummy and blurry eyes.
                                        I spilled lemonade

Open your mouth, he said   Sour breath
and dirty teeth   Confusion and disoriented thoughts
            I cried so much my dress got soaked

Don't want to, she whimpered.   Shame and
fear in ocherous eyelet,   Standing in acrid warmth.
                    I was watering the garden

You are dirty now, he said   And you stink
Pink and green flowers stained yellow.
                    I don't know what happened

It's not my fault, she says   Rinsing off with the green garden hose
     Trying to wash off the uncleanness.   Wet pungence on young limbs
Everything silenced   Running away in the evening dusk

-Valeka Cruz

Red Handed

-Valeka Cruz

The Illusion of Space and Time

Breathe.
The smell of your light
and every secret hidden in your ultraviolet waves
call me to your darkening sea.

The fold of your arms,
The folds of your waves
strike like salty punches.
Memories setting along with the sun,
riddled as the tide.

I still stand where you left me,
where I reached for your stars.
Waiting for your soul to return
with unbent truths.
But I do not question it anymore.

Exhale.

-Ernesto Dueñas

Arribada*

Today is the day.
Brown and green anchors to our world
led by beacons in their heart.

Longing for calm
longing for peace they carry on.

Transcending tides
Transcending waves

that bring them to our dryland
during this, their season.

Today is the day
that gives birth to hope.

-Ernesto Dueñas

* Arribada is the Spanish word for "arrival by sea", the natural phe-nomenon of nocturnal mass nesting by Kemp's Ridley and Olive Ridley sea turtles. First observed by the scientific community in 1961, by producing over a million eggs ashore sea turtles can en-sure their survival even after predation occurs.

José, Can't You See?

José can't you see
as the dawn turns to dusk.
How so proudly we have failed,
as the media keeps screaming…

    THE VIOLENCE IS COMING!
        THE VIOLINS ARE COMING!

    Along with mariachis singing in their star-spangled sombreros,
    pledging their grievance to the flag.

José can't you see?
We are simply one nation.
divinely divided over God.
His grace invisible,
with liberty and justice for none…
of you.

José can't you see?
this land was made by you and me.

-Ernesto Dueñas

Geometry

The triangle is of hope
joining worlds together
holder of secrets gently kept.

A triangle of love for one
citadel warm and safe
it shows the way to eternity.

A pyramid in a fertile oasis
it stands taller than Everest
in a perpetual prayer.

Perfection in blue steel
cold as ice into the cosmos
it is yet the source of all life.

Covered in burning snow
it answers the call of men
refuge to lost souls.

Mathematical assurance of science
it is soft as a diamond
receptacle of infinite light.

The universe under control
it is you, mother of all creators
invincible trinity of eternal births.

-Fabrice Poussin

Making Love with the Stars

Why does the expectation continue on
just a small portion of an anticipated day
when all things must at last come together?

Perhaps the odd routine could end
only if they knew another way
to feel a longing far from the fire.

Entwined in the embrace of the other
the stranger thinks of Picasso
the cruel distortion of lasting pain.

Lost in the depth of faraway stars
vaguely touching a counterpart
they know another ecstasy.

Needing nothing more than a gaze
a nod and a smile within a heaving breast
they walk in the comfort of a great night.

Tomorrow will continue
fueled with the eternal hunger of the cosmos
as they commit to making love with the stars.

-Fabrice Poussin

The speed of infinity

I have traveled at the speed of light plus one
chasing visions beyond the home universe
listening to an infinite symphony.

A myriad of notes danced on rays of fire
and I swirled amid this melodious dream
unlikely dancer in the solace of all knowledge.

Recalling billions of colors from renewed memories
I imagined the gardens of my youth
mixed with tears and fluttering butterflies.

Surrounded by furious winds carrying lethal hail
I was safe as the seven-year-old on his way home
aware of the great haven awaiting.

To know that there was to be no end to the journey
within a perpetual euphoria of the senses
I thought what a wonderful dying this had become.

-Fabrice Poussin

Bonita

Quizá lo que te diga te haga sonreír,
pero es la única forma de tenerte;
sonrisa de viento, ojos de cielo.
Subís en silencio los recuerdos
y todos los días venís desde el ayer.
Y aún te sueño, como un dulce dolor, como una espina.
Quiero olvidarte y volar, y no he podido levantar el vuelo.
Criatura del mar,
Bonita.
Quise quedarme con vos
carita de playa, pelo de arena.
Una noche de amor no alcanza
para llegar al cielo.

-Daniel Frini

Elegía para José, que fue mi abuelo

Al fin me decidí y logré poner en orden las palabras para hablarte.
Pude descifrar lo ineludible de tu muerte.
Encontré el justo equilibrio entre ayer y tristeza. Y entonces entendí
dónde has ido.
Supe que en todos los caminos, en cada grano de arena
tenés un pedazo de mirada.
Supe que sos gigante.
Supe que creciste.
(No sé si vos subiste o Dios bajó, pero creciste).
Sé que somos vos, que sos anhelo.
Que cuando el sol se ponga rojo hacia la tarde, tus prodigios,
tan humanos, hablarán de vos bajo los cien paraísos de tu patio.
Que cuando el viento encuentre, por fin, su música
será porque vos lo has ayudado.
Es difícil de entender, pero he sabido
que algún día, al final
las estrellas escribirán tu nombre en un pedazo de cielo.

-Daniel Frini

Árbol genealógico

Mi columna está construida sobre una maraña
de viejas cargas;
a veces, cuando respiro,
me duelen los anhelos de mi abuela,
esos que viven aquí, en alguna parte de mi   piel,
suben lentamente hasta las angustias y
se duermen al lado de los sueños de mi madre,
las palabras de mi hermana,
los enojos de mi padre.

Desde mis ojos,
no distingo entre mi mundo
y el de los otros,
las aguas que fueron tierra y luego raíces,
las casas que cambiaron de sitio
hasta encontrar cimientos.

Aquí, al final de las ramas,
 mi pelo trenza historias
que aún no se cuentan
y hebra a hebra,
borra las fronteras
que antes se cruzaron.

Soy toda de estos otros
 y a veces, no reconozco
qué ilusiones persigo,
si soy o fui, si debiera ser.
Tal vez, al igual que yo
todos somos, también los otros.

-Guadalupe Meza Servin

Breakup

And what do you know about leaving?
About starting again?
About what you left behind?
About hitting the road?
About hitting rewind?
About setting someone free?
About setting off a bomb of isolation?
About letting go?
About letting time mend a broken heart?
About being alone?
About being friends?
About being in love?

-Daniel García Ordaz

This Is Freedom
A Reinvented Blackout Golden Haiku

(After Paulo Freire)

Freedom (obviously):
Reality dictates that
teaching young learners

reading is not just
eagerly waiting for an
epiphany, Word?

Everything is not
Inherent. Reading the World
and the Word (true lit)

is rarified air.
Wanton waves of struggle, mis-
-pronunciation,

latent letters trip
readers,   but patterns emerge,
illiteracy

sloughs off. New creature
born. Development takes time.
Literacy is

Praxis—not lone skill.
Conversation awakens
Heart revolution:

Anti-oppression
abhorrent to ignorance.
Critical reading

capacity is
the ultimate goal: a re-
invention free from

colonial   ism.
Youth grow in literacy:
This is freedom. This.

-Daniel García Ordaz

I Hear América Cantando

I hear América cantando, the deliciously diverse canciones I hear.
The custodian's canto, sweeping her merry blues in zigzag
staccato between classes, or down empty hallways after school.
The DREAMer's melancholic melody, quietly tuning her cello backstage,
yearning for the day she will show the world the true sound of freedom.
The Afro-Latinx man's cumbia beat, a contagious conga rhythm,
a throbbing connubial pulsation, the percussion of the persecuted,
played from tenement windows, or public beaches.
The cafeteria lady's salsa shake, her merengue mix,
surreptitiously stirring sazón into the Melting Pot,
counterclockwise, to the beat of a different newcomer.
The mariachi band at the bar, singing a son or ranchera,
sorrowful lyrics, infused with furious violins,
campesino compositions granted by floricanto muses,
with choruses sung by the crowd.
Cada uno singing lo que le dé la gana—
whatever their heart desires, whatever they damned well please—
the song of the Coquí, the cricket, the chachalaca, the cenzontle,
the coyote, the cascabel, the carcacha, the cartucho.
Each singing songs of love. Songs of revolution.
Songs of the past. Songs of evolution.
We, too, sing, América.

-Daniel García Ordaz

Virgin Forest

I wish to grow a virgin forest
In my heart.
Let all seeds take roots to the core of it.
And years after years, they may grow to the blue.
I wish, no technology should intervene its pure soul.
Nothing glittering be out in the sun.
No books, no education be allowed inside
To spoil its naturally flowing love.

I know, the warmth, the water makes the seed open its heart,
To pierce the delicate tentacles
into the hard rocks.

This world has frustrated me
By its super-egos touching the skies.
Nowadays, the rain is also acidic...
Full of bile in them.
So, one day, I will sit
in the corner of my heart,
And will let my soul dissolve in that virgin forest
Full of love.

-Tejaswini Patil, Ph.D.

Muse and Music

Passing through
The long passages of darkness
Towards you,
I'm lighting these tiny lamps
On every difficult turn
And placing a lyre
Played on the strings of silence.
The generations unable to cross
The lands of the skin;
Deafened by the sounds
Of bullets and screams;
Dazzled by the blinding booms;
Rooted in uncertainty,
Will come this way
Searching for these calm lighthouses
To sleep with the Muse and Music.

-Tejaswini Patil, Ph.D.

Lamps

Look, I have scattered
All my memories,
Carefully saved for years,
On the winds...
In the hibernation,
They have taken
Beautiful colours
Of the rainbow...
I know, they will be
Lamps on my path...
And I will collect
Their light in my lap
Again…

-Tejaswini Patil, Ph.D.

Por la Madrugada: dream cats, birds, and tacos

⇒Por la madrugada. you are visited. by lost loves trying to be found. they present themselves. in attitude. and *why'd you leave me's. when you comin' back*? you do not pay attention. instead watch grackles. as they bathe in the canal. the feral cat. you call *TwoFace* is bathing in the dirt of the driveway. in the cornfield across Breedlove road. you hear birds who should be asleep. singing a song that should be played on cello. low and moaning. and you worry they portend something darker. than this night coming. but then think. why is dark always associated with something bad or scary. you say aloud. *that's odd*. and isn't what they're all doing something they normally do during the day? Or is it the way they act when they think no one's looking. but you are. you see it all. the star road is clear tonight. but you don't wish. because you stopped wishing on stars. a long long time ago.

Sleep has gotten into the car and gone on to Corpus Christi. so you get out of bed. click on the four book lights you keep clipped like birds perched around the laundry room. the place where you sleep. or at least dream. you sort your clothes again. into two different suitcases. and several recyclable shopping bags. you go right outside the door where your jeep is parked. organize the trunk of your car. TwoFace is still wiggling and wobbling in the dirt of the driveway. Your car has become a third home. or is it a fourth? you have so many houses. and none at all. all eyes are on me. stars peering down from the sky and all I can ask is *why*? then yell up, *can tacos really heal*? can tacos replace the nobel peace prize. can tacos unite the U.N. that's been divided. since the US decided to take its marbles and go home. though it still shows up for meetings. and thumbs its nose. are tacos a universal language? a melding of cultures. beef, pork, or chicken on a tortilla de maíz. Things the colonistas brought to *the new world*. world that was not new at all. it was only new to them. it was pristine. and all I can say is. in my secret dream heart. the taco I prefer is wild *jabalí*.

-Odilia Galván Rodríguez

Higher Respiration. Standing.

Our words get caught and lost in our throats. later we find and dislodge them. we sometimes break out into a terrible roar. then we want more. ways to scream and cry. rage. and say *see me*. no one ever does. they left me abandoned. in corners of rooms. until they needed to use me. to parade me out. as a beauty. a daughter. a fresh thing. to their *been there done that*. around the block too many times. I've been a prisoner of wars. since before I was born.

later. after I escaped. I learned to use my words for others. who too have been muted. told stay quiet or die. *calladita te miras más bonita* — the real message there. just shut up or you die. you out there on the frontlines. tryna be a microphone. a bullhorn. in a world of I see you. but you're an invisible.

of the ones who pick crops. in fields hidden from view. look at all that flawless produce they pick. not at all blemished like you. you're a daughter of those. those who dish wash. dishes that make more noise than they do. of the ones who wash and iron clothes. rock other's children to sleep. who kiss away their tears. their ow-ies. of those who stranger's children call out to in the dark. during their worst night-mares. and for why? where are their parents?

where are the worker's children? who holds their hands? who reads them bedtime stories? or sings to them. while rubbing their backs 'til they fall asleep. you're of those car people. wash cars. park cars. drive people in cars. who weed lawns. who cut grass. who trim trees. who cook food. who build buildings. houses. who build bridges. and walls our kind shouldn't cross anymore. those who are always on their knees. doing something.

and no. no one really sees them. no one remembers. they're always beneath. not at eye level. only on top if *they* say so. and you know. they pick their tokens. just a few. to represent. more like them than us. but these. who represent. say and do all the right things. they've gone and graduated from their schools. they are articulate. know how to kiss ass. if they have to. they are acceptable. and there's only a few. mind you. they a tolerable shade and shape. they look little like our kind. but more like them.

the ones *they* accept. to fill this or that quota. photo op. ones that are vocal. intelligent. kind. know how to smile and speak. but not more than *they* want them to. only say things that make *them* look good. decent. and never shame *them* for their privilege. for their killer instinct. their DNA. for having more. being more. being superior.

some of our words are written. then slammed shut. in pages of books. and because we want to appear civilized. we rage no more. rage no more. we stay behind those ivory tower doors. of academia. toe the line. get in line. for tenure. for awards. for nods. and smiles of *their* approval. for invites. for an attagirl or boy. for them to say. one more time. *you're so much more. and more better. than your kind.*

you understand. it's better. to be better. to get along. to toe the line. better than to end up at the end of one. dangling. out there. all alone. or from a tree. but I say. if I have to die for my mouth. let it be face down. in fields. or in a forest. up in a 900 year old cypress tree. not on my knees. I know who my ancestors are. where I come from. now. I am standing.

-Odilia Galván Rodríguez

Wardrobe for Pandemia

My gunmetal New Balance sneakers,
a tiny silver cup filled with smoky quartz
on my thumb, and a diamond pear nestled
in a cage of white gold on my left hand,
connected by an artery, it seems,
directly to my heart.

I get to school too early
today, I wear the dark like my favorite sweater,
I wear Starbucks Café Americano on my lips,
the morning moon shines silver in my cup.
I sit in my car in silence, and I revise
today's lesson plans.

Today, my students and I will dress in sonnets.
We will dive into Laura and Petrarch,
we will wear iambic pentameter
in the claps of our hands, in between
the beats of our hearts. We will sing
quatrains and octaves.

I wear my black mask as I walk into
my silent classroom. My students wear half-smiles
as they log into my Zoom class. We are all
wearing trials underneath our clothes,
a private hairshirt whose itch we cannot reach.

Today, we all show up. We all try.
Even if we sometimes forget what we're trying for.
We all wear a cloak of sadness, heavy as plague…
But we try. Today we will wear poetry,
try to make rhythm of breath,
try to forge wings out of words.

-Lucinda Zamora-Wiley

This is Jeopardy! (On the Occasion of the Death of Alex Trebek)

He left work on Friday, said he'd be back
week after next...he was gone
by Sunday. I watched his final episode,
surprised, as he likely was, it was his last.

What is a soul whose heart is visible
in his eyes? What is the reason why
my father and I can speak to one another
while we play, sitting together on one couch?
What is a conduit for love between
father and daughter? What is an antidote
to Vietnam and PTSD and silence?

Now that I've lost you, I feel like I've lost
a bit of my own family, my father, too. . .
He is back to silence, and there is no more time
for games we used to play. Dad's Parkinson's
grabs and grips, the trembling shakes him,
shakes me. I can hear the rattling of his heart.

What can I say after his second brother
shoots himself? What can I speak
that will pierce the silence between us?
What can I do when the only answer
is more questions?

-**Lucinda Zamora-Wiley**

Youth Poets

Silhouette

sometimes I wonder if you think of me
the way children think of the sky
with wanderlust and oblivion
about what's beyond the blue abstract void
silhouette
dressed in a milky elegance.

or maybe I remind you of the moon
and how she sits on her throne in the sky
overseas of silk
greased slip nights
drifting, driftwood
the sky is decorated
until velvet morning.

-Heaven R. Navarro

nuchal cord

dark circles and Indian smiles
dreams disappear like clouds of opium smoke
children laugh like fanfares of music
surround us
surround us and settle like dust
amongst prairie homes.

I often find myself
scared and alone
walking through corridors crafted by scars

I stare into the face I hate
I bite the hands that feed me
I'll suffocate the face that breathed hatred into my lungs
Ink unto my umbilical cord.

-Heaven R. Navarro

Oh, my baby!

Dedicated to my aunt

Oh, my baby!
You have grown lately!
I cannot stop thinking
about you. I cannot wait
till you're due. The first time
I felt you kick, I felt nothing
but a little flick. Oh, my baby!
Soon you will be running
around the house.
You will not
be as quiet as a mouse.
Taking your first steps will
bring me great cheer. Oh, your
Grandma will be happy to hear!
I feel you moving inside. Maybe
you are dreaming you are on a
roller coaster ride. My, whose
features did you take? Will you have
your father's sweet tooth for cake? Will
you have my cute button nose? Soon I will
be cleaning between your toes. Oh, my baby!
You will be so tiny in my arms. Admiring your
charm. I am nervous, my baby, for when you are
born. The pain you will bring, I shall be warned.
My, I will be a mother to you with my love. My
pure baby dove. You will beam so bright like a
sunflower. Oh, your aunts will make
us both a grand baby shower.
One day my baby you will
see me. God made us to be.
Our encounter will be
magical like Cinderella.
Oh, my baby Rosabella!

-Bernice Zavala

La verdad

Es difícil aceptar cuando se han ido.
Esa es la verdad.
Mi miedo me devora como si fuera
un plato de comida.
Perder a alguien es como perder
pedazos de mi corazón.
Poco a poco me empieza a afectar
hasta que tiene el control total de
mi cuerpo.
Nunca podré aceptar que ellos se
fueron. Nunca.
Ese es mi miedo.
Aceptar que se han ido.
La verdad.
La verdad sobre mi miedo de aceptar.

-Prisma Salinas

The Light I Have

I see a light on the other side.
no matter the attempts to process or visualize
the overwhelming luminosity prevents the eye from the slightest grasp.
all I know is that it is bright.

Imagination and dreaming will lead themselves where they please
life is a reality and dreams may remain as dreams
I will not limit the possibility of feeling the warmth of my light
inching forward so that I could eventually encounter it
an unknown, yet certain, possibility reveals itself as the source of radiance

What emits does not find itself to be an individual or any object
rather, it is a certain, infallible piece of knowledge
a fact that I will hold true and that will be true
this light will never dim, no matter the circumstance
with attempts I make to reach my destination

Obstacles may, and will, shorten my perceived magnitude of white
obstacles are realities, but none that I cannot surpass
the light will always be as present as it always has
just as sure as this, is progression in steps and grasping

Once the journey has concluded,
will I feel the hope for, yet doubted a few times, reality of my future
certainly, I will even come to only ever brighten the light ahead.

-Adrian Flores

An ode to my grandmother

The oldest of twelve siblings left to be self-reliant
A woman who broke the chains of what society deemed "unacceptable"
A single mother left to fend for her only daughter
A woman who climbed mountains towards success

Skin tan and wrinkled around her face
Her hands have leathery feel to them that have seem to age gracefully
Her hair an auburn red with tight coiled curls almost like an afro
Her arms around me are a blanket that seem to shield me from reality
Her eyes brown with a the taint of golden silks
Her whisper is like a lullaby teasing you to sleep

When she speaks you can hear the heavy accent
 pronouncing every "sh" like a "ch"

Her voice dances around every corner
She'll refuse to whisper for her voice has been silenced far too long
Like a rose she has built thorns around her
But what you may find inside is far better

-Jimena Roman

The Earth is Also Alive

They say water is a body and forget the earth is one too
Her heartbeat is too often mistaken for the sounds of cars and sirens

At night, if you listen closely,
You'll hear it beating earnestly
Like a wave of 2am nostalgia
Only when we sleep is the earth at peace

I've known her since I was a child
Playing in the strawberry fields
Where my grandparents once spent hours
Bending their backs just to lift up their children
I was always taught to respect both of my mothers
Though Mother Earth never speaks in words

She speaks through the rumbles of her belly
And the whistles from her cherry red lips
Every gust   a hush
Every tide   a lullaby
Listen when she calls you to embrace her

Soak in every inch of nature's beauty
The fields   her rib cage
Every strawberry   a blood cell
Growing in abundance to fuel her *corazón*
We are not the only ones fit to live in this universe
La madre tierra también tiene cuerpo

Too often she is ignored by us
When we turn to our phones instead of out the window
And dig into our meals instead of our gardens
We must look out for the signs when she cries for us
After all la madre tierra no habla con palabras

So I hope you know that while you dance in the rain
She is only trying to make you aware of her pain

-Angelina Leaños

Lovelight

Too often

        I've searched for it in other people

a magnet

      looking for its opposite

          just to feel a pull that means attraction

             intimacy

        just to feel *something*

When I do not love myself

           enough

I hope   more than anything

        that someone still does

After all,   light is brightest in the dark

Love light is something

        I can never seem to find

Rather than looking   into that golden heart of mine

      beaming

        with too much love   to be reflected back

     too good   for my own good

I search for someone else

    search for confirmation of my worth

           in another's heart

            another's eyes

hands outstretched in the dark   wanting nothing

            but that something

that can only be found

      in the love light

          inside of myself

-Angelina Leaños

Please don't touch

My body is a work of art
Created from generation to generation
I do not need your contribution to be complete
I am already a masterpiece
I am not flattered
By the way you look at me
Your gaze does not make me smile
I have seen too many people like you
Searching for an easy way in and out
But you will not find get that with me
I will not let you near me

Please don't touch
My body is not an empty canvas you can stain
With those greedy hands of yours
I do not want your colors on my skin
You see, whatever you do to me
Could never be washed away
You are not the invisible ink you think you are
You are a permanent marker bleeding
Through pages of literature
You do not get to touch art without
Leaving your tracks behind

Please don't touch
My body is a priceless artifact
There is a reason the signs are everywhere
I am worth more than you could ever afford
I don't even know if I can recover
From the damage if you do   so
Please don't touch

-Angelina Leaños

Desvaneciendo

Cada vez que es noche
El respiro
Para
Los pensamientos
Sobrellenan
Las lágrimas
Caen
La luz oscurece
Queriendo correr
Queriendo enfrentarlo
Queriendo respirar
Queriendo gritar
Queriendo sentir paz
Queriendo sentir calidez
Corro
Y corro
Veo al final
Corro y corro
Y no llego
Siento que todo se está derrumbando
La voz en mí grita:
¡Corre y no mires hacia atrás!

-Isabel García

Fading

Every time its night
The breathing
Stops
The thoughts
Overfill
The tears
Fall
The light darkens
Wanting to run
Wanting to face it
Wanting to breathe
Wanting to scream
Wanting to feel peace
Wanting to feel warmth
I run
And I run
I see the end
I run and I run
And I don't get there
I feel like everything is crumbling
The voice in me screams,
"Run and don't look back"!

-Isabel García

Imperfect and Flawed

You do not know what it is like behind these blinding lights,
The fake mask and the never-ending smiles always become a blur.
Never knowing who to trust, what with being betrayed too many times to count,
Never letting your guard down in fear of being hurt once more.

Caring hurts too much and in return you become left with more than you can handle,
Happiness seems so far out of reach and I am too broken to even attempt it.
Love is a bottomless pit of despair that will just consequently ruin you,
It makes you vulnerable and weak beyond comparison.

Pain and suffering consume me beyond anything that I have ever felt before,
I love too easily and my heart slowly fractures piece by agonizing piece.
I cannot be the person people want me to be without losing a part of myself in the process,
There is more to me than first meets the eye.

I love and hurt easy, I make countless and various mistakes,
But in reality, that is what makes me beautifully human.
I live and I learn, which makes me perfectly imperfect,
I possess this inner flame that always ignites inside of the person that I was meant to be.

-Emily Lara

Time

I sat there

I waited

I believed

The trees grew around me The moon was hidden from me Time

moved on without me I sat there

I waited

I believed

I grew old

But you never came

-Rodrigo Fernandez-Esquivias

eñd

       Where are you from, they ask Your accent is weird
Your name is too long
Your people are feared
Get out of our country
They say so bluntly
Hop back on your boat
Jump back over the fence
Stop stealing our jobs
       Your words aren't making any sense -
I just want this
To eñd

-Rodrigo Fernandez-Esquivias

Who Am I?

I do not know who I am.
I feel like I am a lost soul trying to find a purpose.
I do not know who I can trust.
I feel like no one needs me.
I do not know what I am doing in life.
I feel like I will never be successful.
I am not that smart.
I am not that great.
I am not who people think I am.
I am not the person my family wants me to be.
I hate who I am.
I hate that I cannot recognize the person inside.
I hate that what you see on the outside is not what I see on the inside.
I hate that I fail at everything.
I want to scream
I want to cry
Whenever I ask,
Who am I?

-Natalie Viveros

¿Quién Soy?

No sé quién soy.
Siento que soy un alma perdida tratando de encontrar un propósito.
No sé en quién puedo confiar.
Siento que nadie me necesita.
No sé lo que estoy haciendo en la vida.
Siento que nunca tendré éxito.
No soy tan inteligente.
No soy tan bueno.
No soy quien la gente cree que soy.
No soy la persona que mi familia quiere que sea.
Odio quién soy.
Odio no poder reconocer a la persona que hay dentro.
Odio que lo que ves por fuera no sea lo que veo por dentro.
Odio fallar en todo.
Quiero gritar
Quiero llorar
Cada vez que pregunto,
¿quién soy?

-Natalie Viveros

Avanzar

Se siente como si fuera ayer, iba a la escuela y volvía a casa.
solo para dormir todo el día
 poder hacer eso ahora se siente como un lujo
el tiempo que dediqué a los videojuegos y
ahora es el momento que dedicó a la tarea y trato de mejorar mis
calificaciones
dicen que sólo se vuelve más difícil a medida que creces
creo que es gracioso cómo los niños quieren ser adultos
y los adultos quieren ser niños
porque los niños quieren ser libres y comprar lo que quieran
y los adultos quieren que los cuiden y no tener que trabajar
esta parece ser la verdad, por broma que parezca
no lo tengo difícil
y no soy viejo
pero sólo para volver a ser un niño y no tener responsabilidades
haría casi cualquier cosa

- Daniel Gómez

Advancing

It feels like just yesterday I would go to school and come back home
just to sleep the whole day
being able to do that now feels like a luxury
the time I spent on video games
is now time I spend on homework and trying to improve my grades
they say it only gets harder as you grow
I think it's funny how kids want to be adults
and adults want to be kids
because kids want to be free and buy what they want
and the adults want to be cared for and not have to work
this seems to be the truth as joking as it sounds
I don't have it hard
and I'm not old
but just to be a kid again and have no responsibilities
I would do just about anything

- Daniel Gómez

Invisible

Being invisible can be bad or good
It can be good because you can avoid problemas
Or people you don't want to see

You can feel powerful
When you can see others without being seen
You can practically do whatever what you want

It can be bad to be invisible
When the people you love
Who you want to notice you,
Don't notice you

Being invisible means being able to look at things
Without being seen, but that also means
Looking at things you don't want to
Even if they're good or bad

Even if its good or not,
Just the idea of being invisible
Is something that everyone has thought about,
And it's an incredible thought
That you can only think of

-Mayeli Guzman

Home is Where the Heart is

Beautiful little flower that would dance in the wind. Why are you droopy as the sun barely caves in. Was it the way the grass moved, or the way the wind sang. Your gorgeous bright colors now flushed away. A burden is how it feels. Being trapped away in the basement of a house you dare not go into. A house everyone once adored. I envy those with the white picket fence they have all around. And the classic red door with the brick pathway in the front lawn. Sometimes I like to go and walk around those neighborhoods and wonder how it feels. Just to imagine their life and if it has a single flaw like mine. Oh, the wonders and secrets the walls must keep. If only they'd tell how they'd done it. Maybe then I could have my own white picket fence. But for now, I just dream. And I watch from a cracked grayed window right next to the ground, where the spiders find comfort and the rats don't make a sound. Where an old furnace would be, and the little ones are too scared to go. One day the shadows of the basement won't hold me no more. And my own house will stand tall. And the neighbors may criticize and not sympathize with my journey. But it'll be my home.

-Savannah Sanchez

El muchacho que me hace sonreír

Es más delicado que una flor pero
por fuera pretende ser fuerte.
Lo llamo "el chiflado"
tiene una sonrisa perfecta con un pocito en cada lado
y un par de lentes que hacen que se parezca a Harry Potter.
Él es como un niño jugando en todas partes
pretendiendo ser un ninja cuando está aburrido
pero no hay que dejar que la ansiedad lo toque
porque se desaparece sin decir ni una palabra.
Él es sólo un amigo
es lo que me digo a mí misma.
Es más terco que una espina enterrada profundamente en tu pie
pero creo que eso es lindo,
él cree que es alto, 5'9 dijo él
ahora me dice "chaparra" 5'2 dije yo.
Él sabe que me molesta pero aún así lo hace.
Él es sólo un amigo que me hace sonreír y reír todo el tiempo
es sólo un amigo es lo que digo
pero a quién le miento, sólo a mí misma porque
él es el muchacho que me hace sonreír.

-Sherlyn López Jiménez

Una pareja del infierno

Un pareja inseparable, que nacieron juntos

Su hermano de sangre, su pareja de crimen

Cual dominará al otro, comparten el mismo cuerpo, pero diferentes mentes

Uno es malasios similar a el mismo diablo,

Desea todo para él, es orgulloso, egoísta al igual no desea ayudar a nadie

Prefiere que el mundo arda, el sirviente de lucifer y la sombra del otro.

El otro es gentil, amable, dócil y desea lo mejor para otros, es el que domina la víbora de su sombra, es la imagen original que dios deseo para su hijos, los humanos

Pero el veneno del diablo sigue en los humanos, haciendo que cualquier humano nazca con dos mentes,

Los dos hacen una pareja del infierno ya que en los otros dos mundos son con considerados como una pareja del infierno porque poseen un cosa que desprecian Maldad o Gentileza

A couple from hell

-Bryan Beltrán

An inseparable couple, who were born together

His blood brother, his crime partner

Which one will dominate the other, they share the same body, but different minds

One is evil like the devil himself,

He wants everything for himself, he is proud, selfish just as he does not want to help anyone

He prefers the world to burn, Lucifer's servant and the shadow of the other.

The other is gentle, kind, docile and wishes the best for others, he is the one who dominates the viper in his shadow, he is the original image that God wishes for his children, humans

But the venom of the devil remains in humans, causing any human to be born with two minds,

The two make a couple from hell since in the other two worlds they are considered as hell because they pose something that they despise, Evil or Gentleness

El sueño americano

no importa si se trata de la ajetreada ciudad de
Nueva York o las granjas rurales de Texas,
Estados Unidos es un país de ensueño
un país en el que algunos desean estar
un país hecho por la gente para la gente
donde la igualdad es la única política
un país que grita libertad
un refugio seguro para el resto del mundo
un refugio para los desamparados
un lugar donde todo es posible
un lugar sin límites
un lugar ilimitado
el sueño americano

The American Dream

no matter if it's the busy city of
New York, or the Rural farms of Texas,
America is a dream country
a country some wish to be in
a country made by the people for the people
where equality is the only policy
a country that screams freedom
a safe haven for the rest of the world
a shelter to the unsheltered
a place where anything is possible
a place with no limits
a place that's boundless
the American Dream

-Johnny Miranda

VIPF CONTRIBUTORS

Sandra Dolores Gómez-Amador is a Mexican writer, translator, and researcher. She studied English Literature at Universidad Nacional Autónoma de México. Her poetry, essays, and literary reviews have been published in several Mexican magazines. One of her short stories was published in the anthology Microtopias (2020). Amateur ghost hunter.

ODILIA GALVÁN RODRÍGUEZ is a poet, writer, editor, publisher, and activist. She is the author of six volumes of poetry, and editor of one book and three anthologies. Her latest book, The Color of Light, (FlowerSong Press, 2019) is an extensive collection of chronicles and poetry honoring the Mexica (Aztec) and Orisha (Yorùbá) Energies, which she researched and wrote during her time living in Cuba and Mexico. Also, along with the late Francisco X. Alarcón, she edited the award-winning anthology Poetry of Resistance: Voices for Social Justice (University of Arizona Press, 2016). Galván Rodríguez has worked as an editor for various print media such as Matrix Women's News Magazine, Community Mural's Magazine, and Tricontinental Magazine in Havana, Cuba. She is currently the editor of Cloud Women's Quarterly Journal online and facilitates creative writing workshops nationally. As an activist she worked for the United Farm Workers of America, AFL-CIO and the East Bay Institute for Urban Arts, has served on numerous boards and commissions, and is currently active with women's organizations whose mission it is to educate around environmental justice issues and disseminate an indigenous worldview regarding the earth, and people's custodial relationship to it.

FEATURED WRITER Luis Alberto Urrea is a 2019 Guggenheim Fellow, a Pulitzer Prize finalist for nonfiction and the best-selling author of 18 books of fiction, nonfiction and poetry. He's been honored with a 2019 Pushcart Prize, an American Academy of Arts & Letters award and an Edgar Award. His most recent book is The House of Broken Angels, a NYTimes Notable Book of the year, finalist for the National Book Critics Circle Award and recently acquired by the Hulu network for a series. His novel Into the Beautiful North is a selection of the NEA Big Reads program. He is a distinguished professor of creative writing at the University of Illinois-Chicago.

jo reyes-boitel is a poet, essayist, and playwright. jo is also a queer, mixed-Latinx parent working in community, a former music researcher, and novice hand percussionist. jo's work includes Michael + Josephine, a novel in verse (FlowerSong Press, 2019) and the forthcoming chapbook mouth (Neon Hemlock, 2021), as well as the recently produced operetta *she wears bells*. Publications include The Ice Colony, OyeDrum, Huizache, Scalawag Journal, and Chachalaca Review. As of 2021 jo is a member of the Macondo Writers Workshop and begins her MFA with UT-Rio Grande Valley in Fall 2021.

Lucinda Zamora-Wiley-Lucinda is originally from San Antonio, Texas, but she is an RGV transplant of over twenty years now. She is a high school English teacher at The Science Academy of South Texas, and she is enjoying her twenty-first year of teaching. Related to Elena Zamora O'Shea, author of El Mesquite, reading, writing, and teaching are in Lucinda's blood. A former student of Billy Collins and Sharon Olds, Lucinda's greatest honor and privilege is being the mother of revolutionary poet, Ava Sofia Zamora-Wiley.

Javier Fuentes Vargas (Santa Ana, El Salvador). Estudiante de Antropología Sociocultural en la Universidad de El Salvador. Ha participado en diferentes eventos y lecturas a nivel nacional e internacional. Su poesía ha sido publicada en diferentes revistas digitales e impresas de Latinoamérica. Ha publicado: La muerte llegará (Artesanos & Editores, 2019) y Vaho/Mist (FlowerSong Press, 2021)

Kenneth Johnson is a visual artist, writer, and educator living and creating in southern California. He has published infrequently but is now focused on writing and publishing poetry. He writes in both English and Spanish. His work has appeared in Carousel, Written Tales, and Bein Bua Journal.

Robert J. Cavazos is a poet from San Antonio who teaches English at Texas Southmost College and Harlingen High School, and serves as a Teach For America corps member. Robert is a graduate of the University of the Incarnate Word and NC State University's MFA in Creative Writing program

FEATURED POET Julio Serrano Echeverría (Xelajú, Guatemala, 1983) Poeta y artista multidisciplinario. Es cofundador y editor de cultura en Agencia Ocote. Estudió Literatura en la Universidad de San Carlos de Guatemala, también ha tenido formación en cine y artes visuales. Ha sido becario de la Fundación Carolina en España, de la Residencia para Artistas de Iberoamérica FONCA-AECID en México y de la Fundación Yaxs en Guatemala.

Ha publicado varios libros de poesía y crónica, Tierra (Sophos, 2020) Antes del mar (Metáfora, 2018), Estados de la materia (Catafixia 2017), Central América (Valparaíso, 2015), entre otros libros de poesía; además varios libros de literatura infantil, como Dos cabezas para meter un gol (Libros para niños, 2021), Balam, Lluvia y la casa (Amanuense, 2018) y En botas de astronauta (Amanuense 2015). Publica periódicamente ensayos, crónicas y reseñas en medios de la región. Parte de su trabajo ha sido traducido al inglés, francés y bengalí.

Ha trabajado en diversos registros entre el cine documental y la fotografía en diálogo con el periodismo, el ensayo visual, la ficción y la imagen experimental. Varios de estos trabajos ha participado en exposiciones de arte contemporáneo y festivales de cine.

Dee Allen is an African-Italian performance poet based in Oakland, California. Active on the creative writing & Spoken Word tips since the early 1990s. Author of 5 books [Boneyard, Unwritten Law, Stormwater and Skeletal Black, all from POOR Press, and from Conviction 2 Change Publishing, Elohi Unitsi].

Juan Manuel Pérez, a Mexican-American poet of indigenous descent and a Poet Laureate for Corpus Christi, Texas (2019-2020), is the author of several books of poetry including, SCREW THE WALL! AND OTHER BROWN PEOPLE POEMS (FlowerSong Books, 2020). The award-winning poet, history teacher, and Pushcart Nominee, is also a member of the Horror Writers Association, the Science Fiction Poetry Association, and the Military Writers Society of America. Juan worships his Creator and chases chupacabras in the South Texas Coastal Bend Area.

Tamara Al-Qaisi-Coleman is a bi-racial-Muslim writer, poet, and artist. She is the Editor-In-Chief of Defunkt Magazine. A 2021 Desert Nights Conference Fellow, a poet for The Museum of Fine Arts and Houston Grand Opera's event "The Art of Intimacy" January 16, 2020. Publications can be found at www.tamaraalqaisicoleman.com

José Luis García Herrera, Nacido en Barcelona, España, en 1964. Poeta, rapsoda, narrador y crítico literario. Miembro del grupo cultural Versikalia. Fundador de los premios literarios "Ciutat de Sant Andreu de la Barca". Ha publicado 24 libros de poesía.

Eduard Schmidt-Zorner is a translator and writer of poetry, haibun, haiku and short stories. He writes in four languages: English, French, Spanish and German and holds workshops on Japanese and Chinese style poetry and prose and experimental poetry.

Member of four writer groups in Ireland and lives in County Kerry, Ireland, for more than 25 years and is a proud Irish citizen, born in Germany.

Published in over 130 anthologies, literary journals and broadsheets in the USA, UK, Ireland, Japan, Sweden, Spain, Italy, Bangladesh, India, France, Mauritius, Nepal, Pakistan, Nigeria and Canada.
Some of his poems and haibun have been published in French (own translation), Romanian and Russian language.

He also writes under his pen name Eadbhard McGowan.

Marianne Peel - After having taught middle/high school English or 32 years, Marianne is nurturing her own creativity. She spent three summers teaching best practices to teachers in China. She received Fulbright Awards to Nepal and Turkey. Marianne participated in Marge Piercy's Juried Intensive Poetry Workshop (2016). Marianne's poetry appears in Muddy River Review, Jelly Bucket, Gyroscope , among others. She has a collection of poetry forthcoming in 2021 from Shadelandhouse Modern Press.

Lulu Rodriguez - Life! As a writer. Lulú has kept a journal for over ten years now, and only recently thought to publish some of these ramblings turned poetry. Sticking true to her colorful, wanderlust nature, she embarked on a new journey and moved to New York City in hopes of pursuing this wonderful thing called art further. To quote the fabulous

Mary Oliver, "Oh! How rich it is to love the world," writing and feeling captivated by this spectacular city is what currently moves Lulú's spirit. She hopes to convey all of life's intricacies, turmoil, and splendor to you.

Samuel Strathman is a poet, author, educator, and the founder/editor-in-chief of Floodlight Editions. He lives in Toronto, Ontario, Canada.

Megha Sood is a Pushcart-nominated Poet, Editor, and Blogger. Assistant Poetry Editor at MookyChick(UK), Life and Legends (USA), and Partner in "Life in Quarantine", Stanford University, USA. Works featured in journals/anthologies. State-level Winner NJ Poetry Contest 2018/2019/2020, National Level Winner 2020. Website https://meghasworldsite.wordpress.com/

Ruben Pineda - Un escritor joven que se ha dedicado en sus primeros años a desarrollar un estilo poético propio, aceptando que la vida no siempre es agradable, pero que siempre es bella. Ha publicado dos cuentos en antologías de cuento fantástico de México y Perú. Su poesía aún está por descubrirse.

Maritza Sara Luza Castillo (Sara Lucas) Periodista Profesional egresada de la Universidad "Jaime Bausate y Mesa". Ha laborado en prensa escrita, radial y televisiva en el área periodística. Ha escrito para diarios fuera de las linderas del Perú, como " La voz Hispana de New York", "Il Gazzettino Italiano Patagónico", Argentina, "Listin diario.com" de República Dominicana entre otros. Ha sido distinguida con notas en la revista literaria "Life and Leyends" de California

Ali Blanco - I am a single mom, homeschool teacher, and poet. Unpolished, unpublished, undiscovered womxn, author, and actor. A completely imperfect work-in-progress work-of art. Love, Always.

FEATURED POET Taofeek Ayeyemi (fondly called Aswagaawy) is a Nigerian lawyer and writer whose works have appeared in Lucent Dreaming, Ethel-zine, The Pangolin Review, hedgerow, the QuillS, Modern Haiku, Frogpond and elsewhere. He won Honorable Mention Prize in 2020 Stephen A. DiBiase Poetry Contest and 2020 Akita International Haiku Contest among others.

Megan Wildhood is an erinaceous, neurodiverse lady writer in Seattle who helps her readers feel genuinely seen. She hopes you will find yourself in her words as they appear in her poetry chapbook Long Division (Finishing Line Press, 2017) as well as The Atlantic, Yes! Magazine, Mad in America, The Sun and elsewhere. You can learn more at meganwildhood.com.

LaVern Spencer McCarthy has written and published five books of poetry and three books of short stories. She is a member of several state poetry societies and a life member of Poetry Society Of Texas. She has won over five hundred awards for her poetry and thirty two national awards.

Jen Yáñez-Alaniz is co-founder of Welcome: A Poetry Declaration, a platform for refugee and immigrant voices in partnership with the San Antonio, TX Immigration Liaison's Office. Her poetry is published or forthcoming in The Journal of Latina Critical Feminism, Cutthroat: Puro Chicanx Writers of the 21st Century, I Sing: The Body, and Cloud Women's Quarterly Journal.

Dario Oliva - Jurado de certámenes literarios. Coordinador de talleres literarios. Gestor Cultural, creador del ciclo *POESÍA FUSIÓN*. Publicó: *Epígrafes* (2º Premio Pcial. de Poesía), San Luis Libro, Payné, 2008; *Breviario*, Bs. As., PROA, 2011; *Eco-Grafía*, Villa Mercedes,

Rorschach, 2013; *Cronopias*, V. Mercedes, Rorschach, 2014; *Fuga de Luz*, V. M., Rorschach, 2015; *El laberinto de Proteo*, Mendoza, Troya, 2016; *Lengua rota* (1º Premio Nacional de Poesía "Paco Urondo" 2017), Villa María, Córdoba, GPU., 2017; *Lo que aturde* (2º Premio Int. de Poesía SUR-Palpalá, Jujuy 2017), San Luis, Perniciosa, 2017; *Preguntas muertas* (2º Premio de Poesía Jorge Leonidas Escudero, San Juan 2019); y *¡Qué Sé Yo!* (2º Premio del género Infantil, Jorge Leonidas Escudero, San Juan, 2020).

Pedro López Fernández (Cehegín, España, 1966)
Finalista de los Premios Ciudad de Barbastro (2014) Gonzalo Rojas Pizarro (2018) y Enrique Pleguezuelo (2020) Participa en antologías de España, México y Argentina. Autor de las novelas "El Magistrado Cuernavaca" (2014) y "Las cenizas de Manhattan" (2018) ambas con Editorial Amarante.

SAHILÍ CRISTIÁ LARA (Cuba, 1989). Poeta, socióloga y demógrafa. Gran Premio, Concurso de Poesía (2009). Medalla de Bronce, Encuentro de Escritores Universitarios (2011). Medalla de Oro, XXIV Festival de Artistas Aficionados (2012). Primer Premio, Girasol Azul (2013). Primer Premio, Luisa Pérez de Zambrana (2014). Segundo lugar, Concurso Puentes (2020).

Nelson Eric castillo inostroza - Escritor y poeta chileno , escribo bajo el seudónimo de Erick Diez en mi página poética de Facebook.
participando activamente en revistas y blogs de España, México, Argentina y Colombia.
También siendo partícipe de antologías poéticas y narrativas de mi país con mis poemas y relatos breves .
https://www.facebook.com/eryckdiez

Stuart Stromin is a South African-American writer and filmmaker, living in Los Angeles. He was educated at Rhodes University, South Africa, the Alliance Française de Paris, and UCLA. His work has appeared in Sheila-na-gig online, The Chaffin Journal, Garfield Lake Review, The Raven, Immigrant Report, Dissident Voice, etc.

Tali Cohen Shabtai, is a poet, she was born in Jerusalem, Israel. She began writing poetry at the age of six, Tali's poems express spiritual and physical exile. She is studying her exile and freedom paradox, her cosmopolitan vision is very obvious in her writings. She lived some years in Oslo Norway and in the U.S.A. Tali has written three poetry books:" Purple Diluted in a Black's Thick", (bilingual 2007), "Protest" (bilingual 2012) and "Nine Years From You" (2018).

By 2021, her fourth book of poetry will be published which will also be published in Norway. Her literary works have been translated and published into many languages as well.

Christos R. Tsiailis has six published books and many participations in short story and poetry anthologies around the world. He is also a dramatist and is involved in theatre as an assistant director. He is occasionally a judge in literary contests. He occasionally attends literary festivals around the world and is a local municipality literature affiliate.

Don Webb - Mr. Webb teaches Special Ed English at a Title 1 High School in Austin. He also teaches Creative Writing for UCLA Extension. He is better known for Science Fiction and Horror short stories, His work has appeared in Asimov's, Analog, Fantasy and Science Fiction, Interzone and Weird Tales.

Laurie Kolp is an avid runner and lover of nature living in southeast Texas with her husband, three children, and two dogs. Her poems have recently appeared in Moria, The Pinch, San Pedro River Review,

A-Minor, and more. Laurie's poetry books include the full-length Upon the Blue Couch and chapbook Hello, It's Your Mother.

Tezozomoc is a Los Angeles Chicano Poet and 2009 Oscar Nominated Activist and has been published by Floricanto Press, "Gashes!: Poems and Pain from the halls of injustice", a collection of poetry, ISBN-13: 978-1951088040, 9/2019. He has also been published in the following journals: The Oddball Magazine, 06/19/2019. Spitpoetzine, Volume 6, 6/15/2019. The Silver Stork, silverstorkmagazine.weebly.com/, 2018.

FEATURED POET Susan Justiniano-RescuePoetix™, first-generation Puerto Rican Paterson, New Jersey native, has been writing from an early age and, through original works of poetry, essay, monologue and performance, highlights experiences from childhood into adulthood, personal lessons, achievements and moments that require strength. As a bi-lingual artist, she captures the essence of her art with collaborations from all over the globe.
She was introduced and fell in love with Jersey City's underground Arts scene and diversity. RescuePoetix™ emerged in 2011 as an artist, entrepreneur and business entity. While establishing herself as a business, she continued to pursue recording her original works to music.
In addition to embracing artist entrepreneurship, writing and performing at live events, RescuePoetix™ has recorded over fifty original works to music in English and Spanish and pursues a career as a voice actor. As Executive Producer, RescuePoetix™ has harnessed the ability to gather resources across the world into projects that impact souls without barrier.

Mahadma Solís - Mahadma, padre de una niña y dos más, psicólogo desempleado, publicado en una ocasión en una revista de arte local y varias veces en una página de internet.

Mahadma, father of one child and two others, unemployed psychologist, published once in a local art magazine and several times on a website.

Rosa Mendoza-Valencia - A Graduate in Hispanic Letters and Master in Mexican Literature. She is a professor of literature at Universidad Nacional Autónoma de México. She has published poetry, short stories and essays in magazines and newspapers. She is the author of the novel "Winter also comes to the pigeons", next post.

Paul Pineda is a first-generation U. S. citizen of Mexican immigrants. Paul is a son of the Rio Grande Valley, having been born in Mc Allen, Texas. As a youngster, he and his family followed the cotton crops yearly from the Rio Grande Valley to the Texas Panhandle.

He retired in 2017 as a Licensed Nursing Facility Administrator and lives in San Antonio, Texas with his wife. He is a published author and previous contributor to Boundless Anthology. His first book, Valle de Lagrimas: Valley of Tears was published in 2015.

Héctor Limón (Arandas, Jalisco, México; 1990) ha participado en varios talleres literarios, además su trabajo poético y narrativo ha sido publicado en diversas revistas y antologías. Está por publicar su primer libro: "El síntoma del impostor" (poesía, Espina Dorsal, 2021).
Dra. Matilde A. Sarmiento-Arribalzaga - Dr. Sarmiento was raised in Harlingen, Texas after immigrating to the United States from Mexico. Her writing is influenced and shaped by the stories her immigrant students share with her. She believes that through writing, a person is able to document and hold on to their culture, define their identity and above all find their voice.

Ndaba Sibanda - Sibanda is the author of Notes, Themes, Things And Other Things, The Gushungo Way, Sleeping Rivers, Love O'clock, The Dead Must Be Sobbing, Football of Fools, Cutting-edge Cache, Of the Saliva and the Tongue, When Inspiration Sings In Silence, The Way Forward, Sometimes Seasons Come With Unseasonal Harvests, As If They Minded:The Loudness Of Whispers, This Cannot Be Happening :Speaking Truth To Power, The Dangers Of Child Marriages:Billions Of Dollars Lost In Earnings And Human Capital, The Ndaba Jamela and Collections and Poetry Pharmacy. Sibanda's work has received Pushcart Prize and Best of the Net nominations. Some of his work has been translated into Serbian.

Ignacio Ibarra is from the Juarez/ El Paso borderland. He attended Bowie High in El Paso and UTEP while living in Juarez, crossing the border everyday, fueling his desire to write. His goal, both as an archaeologist and writer is to tell a more equitable history of where he's from.

Danny P. Barbare has recently appeared in Boundless. He resides in the Upstate of the Carolinas with his wife, family, and sweet dog Miley. He has a deep Southern accent having never traveled far. But his poems have appeared locally and abroad. Including recently in The Pennsylvania Literary Journal, North Dakota Quarterly, Plainsongs, Glass Mountain, Birmingham Arts Journal, and numerous other online and print journals. He works as a janitor at a local medical clinic. And attended Greenville Technical College.

Originally from Ukraine, **Askold Skalsky** is a retired college professor living in Frederick, Maryland. His poems have appeared in a number of magazines and online journals in the USA as well as in literary publications in Europe, Canada, Australia, and Bangladesh.

Sarah Joy Thompson is a Filipina-American author, who has written two poetry collections "The Everyday, the Mundane, and the Brave" (Finishing Line Press, 2019) and "Driving into Black Mountains" (FlowerSong Press, 2020). Thompson's poetry invites readers to reflect on love of family, the thrill of discovering one's true self, and the circle of life – namely our connection to the natural world and its remote landscapes. She attributes her passion for poetry and storytelling to her childhood in the Philippines and her travels to National Parks around America during her days as an undergraduate, while she was earning a Bachelor's degree in English from the University of Texas at San Antonio.

Seeing the world as a poem, Thompson writes about encounters in her everyday life, her travels, and the immeasurable experiences that come with being a mother. She has occasionally dedicated poems to her spouse, son, siblings, and parents, with whom she shares a strong bond. Over the past ten years Thompson has taught ESL online and worked as a communication mentor to develop English training material for call center agents based in the Philippines. She is presently pursuing an M.F.A. in Creative Writing at the University of Texas at El Paso, where she hopes to grow as an author, while exploring new projects in prose and hybrid forms.

Esther M. García (Ciudad Juárez, 1987) es una poeta y escritora mexicana. Estudió la Licenciatura en Letras Españolas en la Universidad Autónoma de Coahuila. Actualmente radica en Saltillo, Coahuila. Su carrera literaria comenzó a los 17 años y ha ganado diversos premios y reconocimientos a nivel nacional, e internacional.

Dos de sus obras poéticas, *Bitácora de mujeres extrañas y Mamá es un animal negro que va de largo por las alcobas blancas*, han sido consideradas por especialistas literarios como libros fundamentales para entender la lírica contemporánea en México, así como la gran violencia de género que se vive en el país.

Dušan Pejaković is a student, volunteer, social entrepreneur and author, based in Podgorica, Montenegro. A passionate reader and nature lover. Currently at the position of MA candidate at the Faculty of Political Science, University of Montenegro. Has been expressing himself through the written word from an early age. He writes and creates on a multilingual basis (languages of the Balkan peninsula area, English, Spanish, Italian). Published so far in several books of poetry, culture magazines, as well as via online platforms and has won many awards and recognitions for his literary work. In July 2020, he published a book of English poetry "Unrest of lucidity" which can be found on Amazon as well as other places Amazon collaborates with. He also writes prose, primarily embodied in the form of short stories, novellas and essays. His second book of poetry, written in his native language (Eng. translation: "The silhouette of an unfulfilled dream") has been published in November 2020. He is currently working on a new project, which is underway, and it is a collection of stories. You can contact him at: dusan.pejakovic90@yahoo.com.

Stephen Schwei is a published poet with Wisconsin roots, now living in Houston. A gay man with three grown children and four wonderful grandchildren, he can be a mass of contradictions. Poetry helps to sort all of this out. www.stephenschwei.com

Allison Whittenberg is a Philadelphia native who has a global perspective. If she wasn't an author she'd be a private detective or a jazz singer. She loves reading about history and true crime. Her other novels include *Sweet Thang, Hollywood and Maine, Life is Fine, Tutored* and *The Sane Asylum.*

Jamie Santomasso is an author from Kansas City, Mo. A writer since the age of five, she has recently returned to the literary arts after a 25 year hiatus. Specializing in free verse and narrative poetry, Jamie takes inspiration from both life experience and imagination to paint vivid pictures of love, heartbreak, fantasy, darkness, and other residual works. Her works have received praise for their ability to evoke emotion, paint pictures, and tell stories that the reader can fully immerse and lose themselves in.

Mark Blickley is a proud member of the Dramatists Guild and PEN American Center. His latest book is the text-based art collaboration with fine arts photographer Amy Bassin, Dream Streams.

Creator **Yu-Hsuan Wu** comes from Taiwan. She writes poems, dances, shoots poetic films and creates a public space for art interaction. She tries to create through expressively interdisciplinary way, to integrate different aesthetic experiences. She regards her living as art practice, to establish a completely humanity version from the separated discipline world. She has published seven books.

Stephen Douglas Wright is a poet, author and playwright from Michigan. He holds a bachelor of arts degree from Aquinas College. His poems and short stories have been published in Global Poemic, Harvard Children's Stories, Bengaluru Review, Refugee Review , Michigan's Best Emerging Poets 2019, and Menteur Magazine, and others.

Krzysztof Dąbrowski - Books in USA: "Escape" (2019 - Royal Hawaiian Press), "Anomaly" (2020 - Royal Hawaiian Press) Books in Spain:"La fuga" (2019 - Royal Hawaiian Press), "Anomalia" (2019 - Royal Hawaiian Press) Books in Germany: "Die Anomalie" (2020 - Der Romankiosk) Books in Poland: "Deathbirth" (2008 - Armoryka publishing house), "Anima vilis" (2010 - Initium publishing house), "Grobbing" (2012 - Novae Res publishing house), "Deathbirth and other stories" (2012 & 2017 - Agharta & Armoryka publishing house), "Z życia Dr Abble" (2013 - Agharta publishing house), "Orgazmokalipsa" (2016 - Alternatywne publishing house), "Anomalia" (2016 - Forma publishing house), "Ucieczka" (2017 - Dom Horroru publishing house) & "Nie w inność" (2019 - Waspos publishing house) ANTHOLOGY in: USA, England, Australia, Canada, Poland, Russia, Germany & India. And he published his stories in the following magazines: PLAYBOY (Slovak edition), USA, England, Czech Republic, Russia, Brasil, Spain, Argentina, Germany, Italy, Hungary, Mexico

Raúl Sánchez - Raúl is the current City of Redmond Poet Laureate. He teaches poetry in Spanish through the Seattle Arts and Lectures (WITS) program, also through the Jack Straw Educational Project. In the last three years he volunteered for PONGO Teen Writing at the Juvenile Detention Center.

Tom Murphy, the 2021-2022 Corpus Christi Poet Laureate. Books: *Pearl* (FlowerSong Press 2020), *American History* (Slough Press, 2017), co-edited *Stone Renga* (Tail Feather, 2017) *Snake Woman Moon* forthcoming (El Grito del Lobo Press). writing in *Writing Texas, Concho River Review*, and *Odes and Elegies: Eco-Poetry*. The *Langdon Review's* 2021 Writer-In-Residence.

Trev Wainwright - Known as Trev the Road Poet, he has been a regular international guest poet since 2012 Popular in the schools and among fellow poets, one of the UK's most prolific travelling poets, with a love of poetry and sharing it. Stopped by covid he is determined to return one day.

Carlos Cumpián has four poetry collections: *Coyote Sun, Latino Rainbow, Armadillo Charm, and 14 Abriles: Poems.* He has been a contributor to more than thirty poetry anthologies. He served as an editor of small press journals and books for March Abrazo Press. Cumpián has taught creative writing and poetry through community arts organizations, as well as at Columbia College Chicago, and taught English and ESL classes for 23 years in the Chicago Public School system. His most recent essay, "Learned to Read at My Momma's Knee," appears in *With a Book in Their Hands: Chicano/a Readers and Readerships Across the Centuries* (University of New Mexico Press, 2014), ed. Manuel M. Martín-Rodríguez.

Paloma Martínez-Cruz teaches Latinx Studies at The Ohio State University, is the author of Food Fight! (2019), Women and Knowledge in Mesoamerica: From East L.A. to Anahuac (2011), and is an editor and company member of Guillermo Gómez-Peña's La Pocha Nostra. She directs Onda Latina Ohio and practices Zen.

FEATURED POET Michael Rothenberg is co-founder of 100 Thousand Poets for Change and co-founder of Poets In Need, a non-profit 501(c)3, assisting poets in crisis. His most recent books of poetry include *Drawing The Shade* (Dos Madres Press, 2016), *Wake Up and Dream* (MadHat Press, 2017), *I Murdered Elvis* (Alien Buddha Press, 2020), and a bi-lingual edition of *Indefinite Detention: A Dog Story* (Varasek Ediciones, Madrid, Spain, 2017). An Arabic edition of Indefinite Detention: A Dog Story, trans. by El Habib Louai was published in Cairo, Egypt by Arwiqa Publishers in 2020 He lives in Tallahassee, Florida where he is currently Florida State University Libraries Poet in Residence.

Eduardo Rosero Porras, nació un 15 de junio de 1987, es un médico y autor novel de literatura, género poesía, reside en la ciudad de Quito.

Ha participado en certámenes locales y nacionales en su país, de los cuales ocasionalmente ha resultado ganador, actualmente colabora con varias revistas literarias digitales, y permanece dedicado a su profesión y a la escritura.

Barbarella D´Acevedo (La Habana, Cuba, 1985). Escritora. Teatróloga, graduada del Centro de Formación Literaria Onelio Jorge Cardoso. Obtuvo el Premio La Gaveta (2020), Bustos Domecq (2020), Beca de creación Caballo de Coral (2018). Publicó Alta definición, antología de cuentos, Editorial Primigenios (2020). Textos suyos han sido publicados en Cuba, México, Colombia, Argentina, Canadá, España, entre otros.

Ana Fores-Tamayo advocates for marginalized refugee families from Mexico and Central America. Working with asylum seekers is heart-wrenching, so poetry is her escape. She has published in The Raving Press, Laurel Review, Indolent Books and many other anthologies and journals, online and in-print. Her poetry in translation & photography have been featured at home and internationally. Through poetry, she keeps tilting at windmills.

Soren Ramsey is an American poet, novelist, and musician based in New Orleans. He is currently working to become a mental health therapist. Much of his writing

Marisol Adame is a Mexican American writer from El Paso, Texas. She has a bachelor's in Creative Writing from the University of Texas at El Paso, where she graduated Magna Cum Laude. She's currently pursuing a Bilingual MFA in Creative Writing at UTEP also. She writes poetry and flash fiction.

Eduar Pájaro Peña nació en Cartagena, Colombia. Su seudónimo es

Ángel Yosniel. Sus relatos han sido seleccionados en distintas convocatorias de Hispanoamérica. Actualmente es redactor en Nota Random, Producciones Carballés, colaborador en Misterioso Universo en la Red. Escritor fantasma en HotGhostWriter, y estudia Contaduría Pública en la Universidad de Cartagena.

d. ellis phelps is the author of three books of poetry, of the novel, Making Room for George, and of the blog, Formidable Woman Sanctuary where she publishes fws: international journal of literature & art. She is the founding editor of Moon Shadow Sanctuary Press.

Gabriel González Núñez is the author of a poetry collection titled Ese golpe de luz (FlowerSong Press 2020) and a bilingual chapbook titled El cicl o / The Cycle (Center for Latter-day Saint Arts 2020). He was born in Montevideo, Uruguay. He teaches translation at The University of Texas Rio Grande Valley.

Named State Poet Laureate of Texas in 2015, **Dr. Carmen Tafolla** is an award-winning poet and children's author, storyteller, performance artist, motivational speaker, scholar and university professor.

The author of more than 30 books and a Professor of Transformative Children's Literature at UT San Antonio, she holds a Ph.D. in Bilingual Education from the University of Texas and a B.A. , M.A. , and a Doctorate Honoris Causa in Humane Letters from Austin College. Tafolla has performed her one-woman show throughout the Americas, Europe, and New Zealand, and her work appears internationally in textbooks, newspapers, journals, magazines, elementary school Big Books & posters on city buses, and engraved on sidewalks and museum walls. Tafolla credits the community around her with her inspiration and her training, and says her works are inspired by "ancestors whispering over my shoulder."

(Colombia, Antioquia, 2002) **Daniela Pérez Taborda**, participa hace algunos años en el Taller de Literatura Rayuela que es realizado en su municipio. Sus textos han sido publicados en tres antologías de este taller, en revistas y antologías a nivel nacional e internacional.

Milton Jordan lives with the musician Anne Elton Jordan in Georgetown, Texas. His most recent poetry collection is *What The Rivers Gather*, SFASU Press, 2020. Milton edited the anthology *No Season for Silence: Texas Poets and Pandemic*, Kallisto Gaia Press, 2020.

G.G. (Giana Gallardo) Hesterberg was born and raised in Brownsville, Texas. She published her first book, Stories by the Seashore, in March of 2019. Her second book, Music, Music, You Can Too!, a nonfiction children's book, was released in July 2020.

John Johnson is a writer from McLean, Virginia who focuses his poetry on odd and interesting occurrences in everyday life.

Loretta Diane Walker, a member of the Texas Institute of Letters, is a multiple Pushcart Nominee, and Best of the Net Nominee, won the 2016 Phillis Wheatley Book Award for poetry, for her collection, In This House. She has published five collections of poetry. Her collection Word Ghetto won the 2011 Bluelight Press Award.

FEATURED POET Lt. Sandhya Suri

She is a human being first, an Indian who was born to a Kashmiri Punjabi father and a Nepali mother. Her outlook of life embraces her mixed blood origins. An alumnus of St. Joseph's Convent, Lt. Sandhya Suri is a first generation Navy Officer and among the few to have served on a warship nearly 21 years ago, she moved on to a corporate career across various functions in India and Nigeria, to finally establish her firm in Media, Publishing, Consulting and Events. A TEDx Speaker and Change Enabler, her firm has a separate division called WEPA India for Women Empowerment Project Awareness.

Author of the Military Political Drama Fiction Tryst With Destiny – Abhikrama, her poem We Were Stars was first published in the American Anthology Poetry of Resistance: Voices for Social Justice. Kahi Ankahi, contains 11 of her poems in English and was released at the Global Literary Festival Noida in 2019. Her poems were also published this year in the American Anthology Boundless 2020, released at the Rio Grande Valley International Poetry Festival in April 2020 and one among them got her a nomination to the Pushcart Prize 2020.

She is a bohemian soul with a passion for travel and writing and immersing into zen space with art and creativity. She is currently juggling between diverse activities including a few other book projects, hosting conversations on taboo topics and literary events online.

Her life philosophy is based on ikigai (reason for being), meraki (putting soul into one's work) and insists life is a constantly evolving process and learning never ends. We are all invaluable because each time we have been broken, we have added precious life experiences to our lives and made it priceless. Gratitude in attitude is important.

Erika Garza is from México. She holds a Master's of Arts in Spanish from UTPA. Her poetry have been published in FEIPOL Anthology 2018, Boundless 2019, Boundless 2020, Dreaming: A Tribute to Selena Quintanilla-Pérez, FAME RGV, Flora Fiction, 6to Encuentro de Poetas del Cupatitzio, Tierra Firme and Mariposas sin primavera.

Vanessa Caraveo is a bestselling and award-winning author, published poet, and artist who has been avidly involved in writing throughout the years. Her poetry has been published in various literary magazines and anthologies in which she aspires to uplift the lives of others through her literary work.

Joselin Mejía Garcia. One of her writings appeared in *Teacher's Stories*, a digital project, translated into English and French. Another one of her texts can be found in *Crónica de una pandemia*. La Gata Ediciones, a Chilean publisher, is currently working on an anthology that includes one of her poems.

Sylvia Sánchez Garza's novel, Cascarones, has won several awards. Her poetry has been published by Unique Poetry, Poetry and Covid, The Ana Magazine, and The Indian Feminine Review. Her poems will be available in an anthology by The Ice Colony and other works are forthcoming. She lives in Edinburg, TX.

Sandra Dolores Gómez-Amador is a Mexican writer, translator, and researcher. She studied English Literature at Universidad Nacional Autónoma de México. Her poetry, essays, and literary reviews have been published in several Mexican magazines. One of her short stories was published in the anthology *Microtopias* (2020). Amateur ghost hunter.

Jules Schulman is a LA-based journalist and researcher.

Candice Louisa Daquin immigrated to the American SouthWest and has lived and worked there ever since. Her mixed heritage background (Egyptian/French) and queer identity, influences her writing and when she is not working as a Psychotherapist she is a Senior Editor at Indie Blu(e) Publishing, a feminist micro press. Recently Daquin co-edited with Megha Sood, The Kali Project, a huge anthology of Indian female poets. She also edited Indian surrealist poet Devika Mathur's debut collection Crimson Skins. Daquin was editor of SMITTEN This Is What Love Is, an anthology of lesbian and bisexual love poetry, which won finalist in the National Indie Excellence Awards. Daquin's last poetry collection, Pinch The Lock, was published by Finishing Line Press.

Kara Hollowell is a poet focused on the human condition and the body. She takes experiences often overlooked or shamed and turns them into cemented moments through the written word. She is currently working on her Masters in Creative Writing at the University of Texas at El Paso.

David A. Place is a poet and fiction writer. He is a recent graduate of the Master of Fine Arts in Creative Writing program at the University of Texas-El Paso and has just completed his first novel, a work of historical fiction set in Texas and Mexico in the nineteenth century. David lives in the Rio Grande Valley and much of his work concentrates on Texas history and exploring multi-cultural vantage points.

Julie Matta is an advocate and activist of the experience of being Latin in the arts. Her achievements include her original oratory making it to IHSSA (Iowa High School Speech Association) All-State in Individual Speech, and a National DemocracyWorks essay 3rd place winner back in 2019.

FEATURED POET Kai Coggin is the author of PERISCOPE HEART (Swimming with Elephants 2014), WINGSPAN (Golden Dragonfly Press 2016), and INCANDESCENT (Sibling Rivalry

Press 2019), as well as a spoken word album SILHOUETTE (2017). She is a queer woman of color who thinks Black Lives Matter, a teaching artist in poetry with the Arkansas Arts Council, and the host of the longest running consecutive weekly open mic series in the country—Wednesday Night Poetry. Recently awarded the 2021 Governor's Arts Award and named "Best Poet in Arkansas" by the Arkansas Times, her fierce and powerful poetry has been nominated four times for The Pushcart Prize, as well as Bettering American Poetry 2015, and Best of the Net 2016 and 2018. Her poems have appeared or are forthcoming in SOLSTICE, Cultural Weekly, Bellevue Literary Review, Entropy, SWWIM, Sinister Wisdom, Calamus Journal, Lavender Review, Luna Luna, Blue Heron Review, Yes, Poetry and elsewhere. Coggin is Associate Editor at The Rise Up Review. She lives with her wife and their two adorable dogs in the valley of a small mountain in Hot Springs National Park, Arkansas.

Kamala Platt's poetry collections —Weedslovers: Ten Years in the Shadow of September (2014), On the Line (2010), and Gravity Prevails— document and exemplify a poetics of crisis and of resistance by chronicling manmade calamities and the persistence of hopeful acts in marginalized places on our planet.

Linda Romero is from Harlingen, Texas and has been published in the VIPF *Boundless* anthologies, *Along the River 2: More Voices from the Rio Grande* (VAO Publishing), Twenty: In Memoriam (El Zarape Press), and *La Bloga.* She is a Certified Academic Language Practitioner who provides dyslexia therapy, and is currently working on completing requirements toward her Therapist credential.

Mark Esperanza, an Edcouch-Elsa, Texas writer and poet, currently teaches high school in the US-Mexico borderland city of Progreso,

Texas. His creative work appears in numerous anthologies such as Lamar Press' *Writing Texas, Boundless 2020: the official anthology of the Rio Grande Valley International Poetry Festival,* and *UTRGV Gallery: Literary-Arts Magazine.* Esperanza also has a forthcoming research publication titled "Capturing Flash Fiction: Utilizing Graphics, Family, and Friends to Engage ELL Students" and a fictional piece, "La Llorona de Mile 17."

Noël Bella Merriam is an artist and poet from San Antonio, Texas. Her poetry has appeared in Pecan Grove Review, Cactus Alley, The Revue, The Children of Night, and the San Antonio Poetry Anthology. An educator, she spent many years working as an artist and poet in residence across Texas.

Stan Raines - Former teacher Stan has made his way since retiring as a singer at El Hueso in Brownsville, gadfly everywhere, occasional poet, and constant fool. He is husband to Kathy Raines, father to three living sons and one deceased, and grandparent to handsome and lively Calvin and Zaida Lee.

My name is **Moriana Delgado**, and I am a writer currently living in Iowa City, where I pursue an MFA at the Iowa Writers' Workshop. Please find attached my three poems as well as the cover letter.

Jonathan Fletcher, an alumnus of the University of Chicago, Schreiner University, and Our Lady of the Lake University, has been published in *Arts Alive San Antonio, FlowerSong Press, Lone Stars, TEJAS COVIDO, The Thing Itself,* and *Voices de la Luna.* He currently resides in San Antonio, Texas.

M. Anthony Miranda came of age in the border communities of Southern Texas. He was born in 1974 and was raised in what is commonly referred to as the mid-Valley where upon receiving a Bachelor of Arts in the fall of 1999 took his first teaching job at Weslaco East High School. Much of his experiences growing up in a border town inspire the depth of his writing, choosing often to illustrate the effects of institutional structures as they shape the traditionally marginalized and under-represented border communities where Miranda resides.

Kaitlin Kaiyah Howard is a black, queer and female freelance writer. She is currently pursuing a theater degree at Temple University in her hometown of Philadelphia, Pennsylvania with an expected graduation date of May 2022. Kaitlin's hobbies include creative writing, baking vegan desserts and bike riding.

Kathy Trenfield Raines, a happily retired English teacher, has published poems and essays in Boundless, Interstice, Escuchame, Voices From the Chicho and Along the River 2. She currently writes a monthly column for Port Isabel/South Padre Press's Parade insert, each featuring a different creature from the Rio Grande Valley.

Originally from El Paso, Texas, **Maria Eugenia Trillo**, she has lived/worked/studied in El Paso, Kansas, Canada, Mexico, Arizona, New Mexico, and Texas. She has traveled to Central America. Her first public reading of her poetry was done at the Blue Moon Café in Winnipeg, Canada, She read at the first Flagstaff Book Festival and in Silver City, New Mexico.
Her poems were published by the Latin American Institute at the University of New Mexico, the National Hispanic Cultural Center and Instituto Cervantes, and the American Poets Society.

Laura Andrea Vázquez López is a poet and fiction writer from Carolina, Puerto Rico. Her work can be found in Pussy Magic, Rio Grande

Review and Acentos Review. She's currently pursuing her MFA in Creative Writing at the University of Texas at El Paso.

Kim Denning is a Latina poet from Texas who teaches at the University of Texas at Austin. Her poetry has appeared in Last Stanza Poetry Journal, FERAL, and twice in OpenDoor Magazine. Recently, she murdered romance by winning Versification Zine's Kill Cupid contest. She prefers her guitars loud, with distortion.

Ritika Chand-Bergfeld - Ritika is a lifelong lover of the arts. Her work has been published in the Journal of Undiscovered Poets and in the University of Iowa National Poetry Contest for Social Workers. She lives in St. Louis. When not writing, Ritika can be found in her garden, playing with words.

Jeffrey L. Taylor's first submitted poems won Riff Magazine's Jazz and Blues Poetry Contest. He has been published in di-vêrsé-city, The Perch, Red River Review, Texas Poetry Calendar, and Langdon Review. Serving as sensei (instructor) to small children and professor to graduate students has taught him humility.

Houston, TX native **Tori Hicks** is an educator, musician, and writer currently attending the MFA program at the University of Texas at El Paso. Her previous publications include The Piney Dark, HUMID, and the Subplots bi-annual chapbook. Tori's work includes non-normative poetry, essays, and fiction.

Enedina Irene is a San Antonio raised poet, prose writer, and spoken word performer. Her works have been featured in the Mujer –Centric Zine, St. Sucia, and on the Texas Public Radio program, Worth Repeating.

Valeka Cruz is a writer, essayist, and fledgling poet living in Austin, Texas. Her work has appeared in various online publications and journals.

Ernesto Dueñas is an educator and artist in the Rio Grande Valley and has been published previously in the Pan American (2008), Boundless (2008, 2009, 2010), the Rio Grande Valley International Poetry Festival Anthology, Interstice (2009), an annual literary journal published by South Texas College and Saludos, Vol. 1 (2009).

Fabrice Poussin teaches French and English at Shorter University. Author of novels and poetry, his work has appeared in Kestrel, Symposium, The Chimes, and many other magazines. His photography has been published in The Front Porch Review, the San Pedro River Review as well as other publications.

Daniel Frini (Argentina, 1963). Ingeniero, escritor y artista visual. Participó en varias antologías, en diversos idiomas. Su último libro publicado es "La vida sexual de las arañas pollito" (Color Ciego Ediciones, Argentina, 2019). Obtuvo varios premios, el último el 1er Premio en el Primer Concurso Internacional de Minificción IER/UNAM (Instituto de Energías Renovables de la Universidad Nacional Autónoma de México)

Guadalupe Meza Servin - (Guadalajara, México, 1994) Editora y correctora de estilo, escribe regularmente para Blasting News y Revista Yucatán. Sus textos forman parte de la antología de poesía Extática (Salto Mortal, 2015) y han sido publicados en las revistas: Luvina Joven, Engarce, Áspera, El periódico de las señoras y Signos.
(Guadalajara, Mexico, 1994) Editor and proofreader, she writes

regularly for Blasting News and Yucatán Magazine. Her texts are part of Extática poetry anthology (Salto Mortal, 2015) and have been published in the magazines: Luvina Joven, Engarce, Áspera, El periódico de las señoras and Signos.

Daniel García Ordaz - TEDx Speaker Daniel García Ordaz, also known as The Poet Mariachi, is the author of *Cenzontle/Mockingbird: Songs of Empowerment* and *You Know What I'm Sayin'?* García Ordaz, a teacher at La Joya Early College High School, and songwriter and he's also a founder of the Rio Grande Valley International Poetry Festival and an established voice in Mexican American poetry.

Tejaswini Patil, Ph.D. - Founder Director, Innsæi International Journal of Creative Literature for Peace and Humanity; an academician, poet and social worker; writes about Nature, social issues, feminist sensibilities and her experiences. Four collections of poetry are to her credit. Editor, Tunisian Asian Anthology, Mystical Voices. Thrice selected for prestigious Rio Grande Valley International Poetry Festival, Texas, USA. Included in 25 Women of Virtue. Awards- State Level Mahila Samajratna Lifetime Achievement Award, Ukshi, Maharashtra and 'Master of Creative Impulse' by World Poetry Conference, Bathinda, Punjab.

PW Covington writes in the Beat tradition of the North American highway. His poetry and short fiction have earned Pushcart Prize nominations, and his 2019 collection "North Beach and Other Stories" was named an International Book Award Finalist in LGBTQ Fiction. Follow him @BeatPW on Instagram.

VIPF YOUTH CONTRIBUTORS

Heaven R. Navarro - She is a writer who enjoys dark themes and counterculture. She writes for her own pleasure and to create conversations.

Bernice Zavala lives in Progreso, TX. She is a hardworking eleventh grader at Progreso High School Early College. Zavala is the vice-president of the Creative Writers Club, president of the Medical Health Career Club, and co-captain for the Progreso cheerleading team. Aside from her extracurriculars, she enjoys writing. Writing gives one a chance to show the reader a vulnerable side; the side that is never seen.

Although having focused on mathematics and sciences, **Adrian Flores** was truly exposed to the world of writing through his English class during senior year, making him relatively new to poetry. As short as his time has been with writing, Adrian immediately fell in love and does not plan on stopping.

Jimena Roman, a 14-year-old poet and high school student. Jimena writes her poems from her bedroom, under a pink lamp and a number two pencil. A teenager who decided to write poems instead of celebrating with friends. Her journey has only begun as she continues to explore the power of poetry.

Angelina Leaños is the 2021 Ventura County Youth Poet Laureate and youngest Board Director in California Poets in the Schools' history. In high school, Angelina won the Poetry Out Loud competition at both the school and county levels and has since returned as a recitation coach for Ventura County.

Isabel García is a sophomore at La Joya Early College HS. She is a person who loves to do creative things like decorating or writing poems and dance. She comes from a family of 5 and is the middle one. The way she expresses herself is by writing poems.

Emily Lara is a sixteen-year-old poet from Progreso High School. Reading and writing are some of her biggest passions. Her parents are her biggest inspirations and supporters when it comes to writing. She loves creating a world where other people can relate to and be inspired from.

Rodrigo Fernandez-Esquivias started writing poetry as a 15-year-old while in quarantine in 2020. He focused on personal poems, as a means of expressing himself in a time with few social interactions. As a Spaniard, missing home, living in Utah, I found myself writing many poems in Spanish.

Natalie Viveros is a student at La Joya Early College High School. She was published in *Boundless 2020*.

Daniel Gómez would write in his free time when he had nothing else to do. When other people would play games, go outside and play or would draw. He would sometimes write about some moments in his life. Daniel is a student at La Joya Early College.

Mayeli Guzman is a student at La Joya Early High School. She was published in Boundless in 2020.

Savannah Sanchez - Writing has always been something that came naturally for Savannah. For being only seventeen, the experiences she's had have inspired her writings. As a young writer she hopes others can see themselves in her work as she sheds light on the mindset and issues young adults go through.

Sherlyn López Jiménez is a student at La Joya Early College HS and she is a tenth grader. She lives in Sullivan City and is part of a family of seven people. In her free time, she likes to go skateboarding or write poems and letters.

Bryan Beltrán is a 10th grade student at La Joya Early College. His poetry has been published in Boundless 2020 and Still I Rise Anthology.

Johnny Miranda was born in McAllen, Texas February 14, 2005. He is a student at La Joya Early College High School.

FEATURED ARTIST Matthew Revert is a multidisciplinary artist from Melbourne, Australia with a focus on visual art, writing, music and design. His visual art has amassed a strong following and in 2019, Clash Books released a book of his visual art called *Try Not To Think Bad Thoughts*. He is the author of five novels including *The Tumours Made Me Interesting*, *Basal Ganglia* and *Human Trees*. Reissues of his sought after written work will finally be released starting with his first three comedic absurdist novels in 2021 by 11:11 Press. He has had music released in myriad formats by renowned labels such as Erstwhile Records, Kye Records, No Rent among others. His graphic design work can be found on no fewer than 800 book and record covers. Follow him at Instagram @papercrisis or visit his chronically out of date website: www.matthewrevert.com